No Names
No Faces
No Pain

A Voice from Vietnam

John Kildea

EAGLE EDITIONS
2006

EAGLE EDITIONS
AN IMPRINT OF HERITAGE BOOKS, INC.

Books, CDs, and more—Worldwide

For our listing of thousands of titles see our website
at
www.HeritageBooks.com

Published 2006 by
HERITAGE BOOKS, INC.
Publishing Division
65 East Main Street
Westminster, Maryland 21157-5026

Copyright © 2006 John Kildea

Cover art: *Dustoff* © 2000 Joe Kline

International Standard Book Number: 978-0-7884-4142-6

ACKNOWLEDGMENTS

Cover art **Dustoff That Others May Live** courtesy of Joe Kline of Joe Kline Aviation Art, Gilroy, California.

Photographs courtesy of the Office of the United States Army Nurse Corps Historian, Falls Church, Virginia, the National Archives at College Park, Maryland, and Robert E. Kelly, former operating room technician, 2nd Surgical Hospital, Chu Lai, Vietnam.

Statistics used throughout the manuscript were obtained from **Medical Support of the U.S. Army in Vietnam from 1965 - 1970** as recorded in publication 90-16, Library of Congress catalogue number 72-600264, and from actual quarterly operational reports of the 2nd Surgical Hospital as reported from 1967 through 1968 and maintained by the National Archives at College Park, Maryland.

No Names, No Faces, No Pain

Chapter One

Westward Ho!

The Golden Gate Bridge, I'm sure, was beautiful. Fisherman's Wharf probably was a true delight. I remember riding a cable car and even venturing to Chinatown. Those memories, however, have all but faded, replaced by images of 18 year olds, the stench of urine coming from the doorways in which they slept; teens with scraggly, matted hair, peace signs painted on their faces; and the endless line of fatigue-clad "flower children" chanting, "Make love, not war."

It was at moments like these that I regretted ever going to nursing school, joining the Army, and finally volunteering for duty in Vietnam to "get it over with." It was 1967, and I'd been in the Army for six months. Operating room nurses, like myself, were being plucked from stateside hospitals in ever-increasing numbers to serve their one year tours. As a result, the faces around me were changing constantly. Rather then delay the inevitable, I applied for and received orders to embark in August of that year. And now, after bidding farewell to my wife and kids, here I was - southeast Asia-bound!

San Francisco, because of its location, its airport, and its abundance of motels and hotels, was an ideal stopover for the large number of troops en route to Vietnam. The time here served to ensure that immunizations for diseases such as the plague had been received, that wills were finalized, and that individuals were assigned a seat on a "big bird" to Saigon.

Most of us, however, had assumed that this was simply going to be a plane change as opposed to four days of "hurry up and wait." As a result we had brought little cash, and few had ever considered carrying a credit card off to war. Where to lay our heads and how to pay for meals were now questions that had to be answered in groups of five or six, whose hastily formed friendships ensured not only financial survival, but also emotional support.

Even today I can clearly remember the ride from the processing point to our motel. I had teamed up with four helicopter pilots, now all crammed into a cab, bags we were planning on carrying on the flight on our laps, duffel bags somehow squeezed into the trunk. The motel was no less crowded as we flipped coins for beds; losers slept on two chairs pushed together or on the floor.

The next few days, on the other hand, were a blur, with time spent processing, touring, and trying to visit every bar in Height-Asbury. My roommates, knowing that one in every six chopper pilots would not come home, adopted the philosophy of enjoying every moment of what might very well be their last days alive. Maintaining that enthusiasm would prove to be another matter. With the large hippie population roaming the streets and spitting on the sidewalks in front of you, and with waitresses speaking with folks in the next booth about the "baby killers," patience began to wear thin. These guys began to seriously contemplate revenge on the next person who questioned their willingness to make the ultimate sacrifice so that questioners could paint their faces or sleep in doorways.

That moment arrived in a bar on our last night in San Francisco. On our very last stop, the bartender, his conversation replete with antiwar sentiments, refused to heed our pleas to keep our glasses full. Feeling ignored and treated like second class citizens, anger reached its pinnacle, and all four fly-boys made one last trip to the men's room. As I waited outside the bar they emerged one by one, their wind-breakers bulging and zipped to their Adam's apple. Each stood next to the other on the curb, facing the street, and as if a starter's pistol had been fired, they opened their jackets at the exact same moment. A collection of chains, float balls, and various other toilet flush-tank parts bounced to the gutter. Then, the quartet and I, smiling ear to ear and without saying a word, locked arm in arm and filling the sidewalk from side to side, sauntered defiantly down the street. It was amazing how a little mischief, with a blood alcohol level slightly above any legal limit, served to relieve anxiety and frustration!

Next morning, our last in San Francisco, after sipping the strongest, blackest coffee on earth, we began our final packing for the flight "across the pond." Silently, each of us moved from bath to bed, collecting, folding, arranging, and all the while unconsciously searching for that one iota of reassurance to bolster our convictions. However, the constant swirl of controversy around us made this an all-but-impossible task.

One TV channel was showing President Johnson explaining how the spread of communism left unchallenged in South Vietnam would surely result in the loss of independence of every other country in Southeast Asia. He insisted that while not an all-out effort, an ongoing massive buildup of U.S. forces could stop this domino effect, and that we would defeat North Vietnam handily with sheer numerical superiority. Another channel showed newsreels of anti-war demonstrations of over 100,000 people in New York, 150,000 outside the Pentagon, and others in Washington, D.C. and Los Angeles.

The radio was no less calming. One station had General Westmoreland declaring to the nation that we had broken the will of the north, that we were killing the enemy faster than he could be replaced on the battlefield; that his war of attrition was indeed a success! Another station echoed the voice of Martin Luther King encouraging draft evasion, while another played the number one hit song of the week by the Beatles, entitled "All You Need Is Love."

The events of the rest of the day were a haze. We suddenly found ourselves on a flight to Saigon, now five among half a million being sent to fight the Vietcong and the North Vietnamese Army. Those around us on the plane were officers and enlisted, military police, truck drivers, mechanics, and medics. Most were foot soldiers or "grunts." Regardless of rank or occupation, each face portrayed a sense of uncertainty, a feeling that something unnatural was occurring, that the dream would soon end.

An uneasy quiet filled the cabin during the flight with short, superficial, almost whispered conversations. Chit chat flopped between home and what was to be as men spoke of girlfriends, souped-up cars, wives, children, weapons, and "Charlie." The numerous hours over the

Pacific were broken up only by a short refueling stop in Hawaii, and the many cat naps induced by the constant drone of the engines.

※※※※※※

Few of us had any inkling of our final destination in Vietnam. It was understood that, upon our arrival, branch representatives would assign individuals based strictly on the needs of units throughout the country for a particular specialty. Most of us would be replacing troops rotating back to the "real world" after having served their year. Grunts would also be replacing those seriously wounded or killed in action.

Being unfamiliar with the names of hamlets and cities, however, we had little knowledge as to which assignments we should avoid or possibly request if given the opportunity. We recalled seeing fierce fighting in the Mekong Delta on a recent six o'clock news, and learned from other pilots on board that there were now about 450 helicopter gunships in An Khe. Didn't seem like either would be our first choice, but with no "front lines" in Vietnam, cities like Hue with its impressive Citadel or peach blossoms, or Nha Trang with its pagodas and giant sitting Buddha, probably offered no more safety than Da Nang on the Demilitarized Zone (DMZ) between the North and South.

Suddenly, as if a car had braked hard, heads and bodies gently sloped forward as the plane engines decelerated. The change in pitch signaled the beginning of our descent, and, though barely noticeable, awakened even the soundest sleepers.

Conversations increased in frequency and volume. The aisles filled with men making trips to the restrooms. The upper third of the cabin filled with thick cigarette smoke. Before long we could feel our downward decline. It was then that the "No Smoking" and "Fasten Your Seat Belt" signs were illuminated.

Thirty thousand feet quickly became twenty thousand. Soon we were at ten thousand. Eyes, red from the lingering smoke and lack of sleep, peered through windows into the a.m. darkness searching for the slightest hint of what we faced on this side of the world. However, thick jungle trees, even with bright moonlight bouncing from their tops, refused to reveal what lay beneath them. We knew, however, that hidden below were probably acre upon acre of scorched earth as a result of napalm bombings, mile after mile of tunnels hiding the VC, and certainly the memories of the 30,000 men killed in the war thus far. Deep in the pit of our stomachs we could feel the emotional transition from the relative safety of home to this hostile environment taking hold. We knew it was likely that these feelings could remain entangled in our psyches not only for the next year, but for many years to come.

Chapter Two

Reality Check #1

As our descent continued, all eyes were drawn to the front of the aircraft as a tall, attractive stewardess welcomed us to the "free Republic of Vietnam." As soon as the clapping, catcalls, and whistling waned, she informed us that if we paid strict attention we could learn a bit about Vietnam and what we could expect over the next few days.

We soon learned that we were some 7,800 miles from home and were landing in a country whose borders lay completely within the tropics. We were arriving in the middle of the monsoon season; the dry season not due to arrive until November. Even though it was almost four o'clock in the morning we would be landing at Bien Hoa Air Base outside Saigon amid a pouring rain and the temperature hovering around 85 degrees.

Our geography lesson continued as the stewardess walked through the cabin holding up a map of the country. Though shaped like the state of California, it was only about half California's size, stretching some 700 miles from north to south, and 125 miles at most from east to west. It was predominately a land of mountains, dense jungles, rainforests, rice paddies, and only a handful of roads. We were told that both the terrain and the climate would have profound immediate and long-lasting effects on all of us.

First, the few roads available were difficult to navigate and often controlled by the Vietcong. Transportation to our units, therefore, would most likely be by air, either a fixed-wing aircraft such as a C-130 cargo plane, or by helicopter. Further, since we were landing almost in the center of the country, a trip to even the farthest units would be a short hop, and we could all assume that after a brief, rapid in-processing we would arrive at our new duty station by nightfall.

In the next breath we were asked to draw our window shades to "simply reduce the risk of the aircraft becoming a target." For those of us beginning to put two and two together, our heart rates and anxiety levels rose quickly.

Having heard the horror stories from guys returning on their second tour, our imaginations began to run wild. We could picture young soldiers, their limbs and faces peppered with shrapnel from booby traps. We could smell flesh burned with phosphorous from grenades. We could hear the distinct crackle of an AK-47. Our psychological orientation had begun, and the realization was sinking in that all too soon we'd be smack dab in the middle of a war that until now we had only watched nonchalantly on TV.

******

Disembarking from the aircraft, we were directed to move quickly to the terminal, retrieve our bags, and promptly board buses bound for the 90th Replacement Center. Apprehension continued to be the word of the day as when, willingly following instructions, we noticed that the side and back windows were painted black, and that all windows were covered with steel rods and wire screens.

"Done," the bus driver said, "simply to reduce the risk of becoming a target." Where had we heard this before?

"Why the bars and screens?" we asked.

"The VC like to lob grenades into anything that belongs to us and moves," he said, "and this 'kinda prevents that from happening."

"Not an unreasonable precaution either," he assured us. "Only days earlier, two Vietnamese kids not ten years old walked up behind a jeep, loaded with GIs stopped at a red light, and dropped two grenades into the back seat. Two soldiers died and two were taken to the 3rd Surgical Hospital at Bien Hoa, their fates unknown."

Once at the Replacement Center, initial clearing for everyone included checking dog tags for correct information, including blood type; completing pay records to assure adding combat pay to our entitlements, and exchanging American dollars for "funny money" or military script.

We were than pushed through a variety of orientation movies and brief lectures. Though geared toward the soldier in the field, we found most to be meaningful and important, and at the least interesting and amusing to most of us new arrivals. We learned, for example, that you could prevent malaria by taking a prescribed weekly dose of quinine. Old timers, however, told us that taking the medication caused severe diarrhea for several days, and many of us within earshot decided instantly never to have those "big orange pills" go past our lips.

Other instructors showed pictures of immersion foot and discussed how to prevent it. They discouraged drinking village stream and well water for fear of acquiring viral hepatitis. They talked about the tremendous prevalence of VD, and even lightly touched on the availability of dental care while in country.

Quickly now we were ushered toward small card tables with signs designating units such as the "Big Red One" or the "101st Airborne"; the "1st Calvary Division" or the "Americal Division." At the 44th Medical Battalion table I received a courteous but speedy "Hello," and "Goodbye," followed by a short jeep ride to the office of the Chief Nurse of Vietnam. Here I received my second geography lesson of the day. I learned where in country operating room nurses were needed, and received a thumbnail sketch of the differences between the various types of hospitals, as well as an overview of what kind of working and living conditions I could expect.

I learned that Surgical Hospitals focused their attention on combat casualties received direct from the battlefield. Five, ten, fifteen, or more patients could arrive by helicopter at any time, and a mass casualty environment could persist for many hours if not for days.

In the operating room, orthopedic, general, and vascular surgeons could be operating on the same patient simultaneously. Injuries could range from punji stick punctures through thick jungle boots to high-velocity gunshot wounds of the head or chest. Seen also would be men whose legs were blown away after stepping on a land mine. Others would have been robbed of their sight or have had bones broken or arteries snapped by shrapnel ripping through their bodies following a mortar attack.

A typical workday for the nursing staff was a minimum of twelve hours a day, six days, or more often seven, days a week. The ability to prioritize well and be fast afoot were required abilities of a good operating room nurse here; a weak stomach a distinct disadvantage; a compassionate hand, a must.

Field and Evacuation hospitals demanded no less of a nurse's time or talents. Here, patients transferred from Surgical Hospitals two or three days after their initial injuries or admissions and, with predictable recovery periods, could spend between thirty and sixty days convalescing from their wounds or medical conditions. With approximately 400 beds each, these units could support the large number of troops requiring continued treatment prior to returning to duty, and at the same time free up some of the 140 or so beds at Surgical Hospitals needed to accommodate the never-ending flow of fresh casualties.

Though the operating rooms were extremely busy at these Field and Evacuation units, surgical schedules consisted primarily of "scheduled" cases. Initial treatment of wounds at the Surgical Hospitals prohibited extensive exploration, or closure of extremity wounds, or introduction of grafts or implants, for fear of further introducing contamination in an already-dirty wound. But now, in this cleaner environment, tendons could be retrieved and repaired, fractures reduced and plated, colostomies reversed, and flesh wounds primarily closed. Days could be long and tiring at either type of hospital, and while personally satisfying and professionally rewarding, it appeared those at larger hospitals might be somewhat repetitive and predictable.

Next, I learned that accommodations and what little cultural opportunities there were varied according to the size of the hospital and its location. Larger hospitals around Saigon, for example, offered the possibility of exploring the city, and perhaps occasionally partaking of its nightlife. Quarters might be a single room in a two-story billet with a hot shower and toilet facilities on the same floor.

Then, considering where we were and why, if one rated the facilities at the larger hospitals as "two star" or "three star," one could feel fairly certain that those at Surgical Hospitals might struggle to make the "one star" category. Here, wood-framed screened hooches housed four, five, or six men with a "three seater" outhouse about a hundred yards down the road providing toilet facilities. A gutted 500-pound bomb shell, open on both ends and half buried in the sand, might serve as a urinal. A community shower with water from an elevated bladder might provide water warmed by the sun during the hot months, but pure icy terror during the long, cloudy monsoon season.

There was a critical shortage of operating room nurses in all of these hospitals. In addition, nurses were being recruited to serve in any of the three "MUST" units in country. These "Medical Unit, Self-contained, Transportable" hospitals were air-inflatable, rubber shelters with their own portable gas turbine power sources and the ability to relocate quickly. Because of their mobility, they were used primarily to support specific combat operations and, as a result, were often in less secure, primitive areas. Two of the units had recently been mortared, one taking a direct hit on the officers' quarters, both having sustained major damage to their inflatable elements. The remaining unit, the 18th Surgical Hospital, in anticipation of considerable enemy activity, was reorganizing as an all-male unit for obvious reasons, and was looking for "volunteers."

✳✳✳✳✳✳

When I learned that I was going to Vietnam, I decided to simply gain as much experience as I could from the venture, and give as much as I could to my patients. I wanted to test my perceptions of my own abilities in the operating room, and I yearned to gain combat nursing experience, whatever that was.

MUST hospitals seemed to me to be a preferred target of the North Vietnamese Army (NVA), and again, it seemed to me that they were getting very good at what they did. The odds of being awarded a Purple Heart or being sent home in a box, I felt, were much too high, and this honestly frightened me.

Evacuation and Field hospitals, while extremely important in the recovery of those wounded, seemed far removed from the war. These, I thought, would be a watered-down version, a picture, three days after the fact, of the pain and suffering inflicted on the soldiers in this conflict.

I wanted a front-row view of this war, and Surgical Hospitals, while probably not affording the air conditioning, indoor plumbing, and draft beers of the larger units, could provide the opportunity to give just that. Working day in and day out in an environment where patients only minutes ago had tripped a booby trap, been sprayed by mortar fragments, or felled by a high-velocity bullet would surely present the most accurate, timely glimpse of this conflict. It would also require every ounce of ability in a nurse's body to meet the needs of these men.

Chu Lai, just south of the DMZ and a short walk from the Ho Chi Minh Trail, had recently become a hotbed of activity. The 23rd (Americal) Division, formed to complement the 25th Infantry, the 101st Airborne, and the 1st Calvary (Airmobile) Divisions, were all in place to repel three divisions of the NVA known to have been deployed in the area.

To deal with an expected significant increase in the number of casualties, the 2nd Surgical Hospital was being staffed to deal with the anticipated needs of the unit, rather than the authorized staffing numbers. Emergency Room and Operating Room nurses as well as nurse anesthetists were now vigorously being recruited to meet these demands.

My desires to help meet the needs of the unit, its patients, and the Army Nurse Corps, and my eagerness for the chance to gain a valuable "hands-on" education led to my resounding "Yes" to the request to travel north. It seemed to me a logical choice, one that I assumed would end in about a year if I regretted my decision.

Chapter Three

Welcome To The Neighborhood

The airport at Chu Lai laid to the north end of a massive military installation. Coming in from Saigon, 350 miles to the south, we flew over the entire nine-or-ten-mile-wide complex. Taking turns peering through a tiny porthole on the side of the aircraft, we each eagerly tried to catch a small glimpse of what awaited us.

Bordered on the east by the South China Sea and on the other three sides by jungle and the village of Chu Lai, the base was a checkerboard of hundreds of bustling military units with the implements of war visible everywhere. We could see row after row of armored personnel carriers and even a few tanks. F-4 Phantom jets at a Marine base were taxiing for takeoff. Tarmacs were dotted with Huey and the newly arrived, even deadlier, Cobra assault helicopters. Howitzers and other artillery, silent for the moment, sat poised around the perimeter of the base, stacks of live ammunition and empty shell casings piled nearby.

Muddy roads, drying in a fading late afternoon sun, surrounded neighborhoods of warehouses with tin roofs, mess halls, white smoke pouring from their cooking vents, and motor pools with large puddles of oil soaking into the ground. What walkways there were, stretched between buildings and consisted of the sides of wooden ammo crates, broken down, and laid end to end.

Two-and-a-half-ton trucks transporting troops boldly competed with ambulances, jeeps, and bicycles for what little dry main road there was, because deep, inescapable potholes jarred the heads of drivers and passengers alike. At the same time, men walking and clad in steel pots and flak jackets with M16s flung across their backs defiantly challenged passing traffic for the right to travel the same roadway that took them all from point A to point B and back. Amid it all, however, an occasional "gas station" or hand-painted barber pole outside a PX somehow added a bit of character to the turmoil below.

The village of Chu Lai reminded me of a shanty town with more dogs than people meandering the streets. Dilapidated one-room or two-room wooden shacks lined both sides of a litter-filled dirt road. Many houses had tin roofs, some thatched. Though all had the openings for them, none had doors or windows.

Suddenly, as if reassurance from above that we in fact were not passing through the gates of hell, a giant red cross painted on top a Quonset hut passed beneath the plane. Having heard that the enemy rarely attacked hospitals, the words "safe" and "secure" quickly entered my mind. My pulse slowed a bit; the sweat rolling down my back became a lot less profuse.

The thought that a tin building could somehow isolate me from many of the horrors of this war was somewhat reassuring. At the same time, a tremendous guilt began cropping up in my mind as I stared into the eyes of a radioman, two grunts, and a helicopter door gunner sitting next to me or across the aisle. I knew that hospitals were built in relatively safe areas, and though a stray mortar might come my way, I knew I'd never have to tromp through a jungle, or fear "incoming," or ever get the uneasy feeling that I was in the cross hairs of a North Vietnamese sniper's rifle. Unable to share the relative comfort of my own situation, I anguished over the possibilities of theirs.

******

Touchdown was deafening, but the pilot put the plane exactly where he had to on the very short runway. Within minutes we were in front of the terminal, and before the props had even stopped we found ourselves trotting down the aft loading ramp lowered from beneath the belly of the plane.

"Hey, Butter Bar," came bellowing from a small group of men just inside the terminal. His name was Pete, a rank above me at First Lieutenant, average height, tanned, stocky, and walking with the swagger of John Wayne. His crew cut, neatly pressed fatigues, shined boots, and snappy salute gave the impression that this guy was GI from head to toe, but the firm and genuine handshake that immediately followed his salute dispelled any notion of that. An emergency room nurse, married with kids, and one of the men I'd share a hooch with during my stay in 'Nam, he was, I discovered competent, not cocky, big hearted, a nurse who empathized with his patients all too often, and since his arrival, one who had become dead set against the war.

Pete didn't preach to me or give me a list of dos and don'ts on the short jeep ride to the hospital compound. Instead, he allowed my psychological orientation to continue by simply having me suck in the sights and sounds around us.

The sun had set and the breeze from the night air felt great, but there was no question that a war was going on. Most men we passed were carrying weapons, the unmistakable "whooomph" of outgoing artillery could be heard in the distance, and fiery afterburners caught my eye as a pair of F4s lifted from a nearby runway.

Immediately after passing beneath an archway welcoming us to the "2nd Surgical Hospital" and boasting the care to be "2nd To None," we took a zigzag course through the hospital complex for a quick tour of the place. Signs above screened front doors let me know we were passing the laboratory, x-ray, the laundry, and the morgue, here known as Graves Registration.

A smile came to my face when I noticed that seating in the mess hall consisted of wooden picnic tables with benches attached on both sides, just like those in your back yard at home. I grinned again when I observed three small sterilizers in a covered shed behind Central Supply. Truly unique to combat zones, these units were operated by gasoline, and to protect passers-by, sandbags stood high above and around them as well as around the 55-gallon drums of fuel used to power these units.

Outside hospital wards were men in wheelchairs and on crutches, all dragging IV poles behind them, having a smoke and relaxing. Through the screen windows of the intensive care unit I could see nurses scurrying about, hanging IVs, adjusting traction, and reinforcing bloody dressings.

Suddenly we pulled to the side of the road where we watched a "Dust-Off" medical evacuation helicopter glide to a landing not 100 yards from the entrance of the Emergency Room, its blades screaming as they spun, its red cross clearly visible on the sliding door on its side. To this day I can still see the three bullet holes in one of its front cockpit windows.

Our journey now took us past row after row of hooches teeming with activity. Females were segregated to one part of the compound, enlisted men to another, and finally male officers to yet another. These temporary wooden housing structures reminded me of those pictures of the Levittown, Pennsylvania, housing developments of the 1950's minus the manicured lawns and driveways, of course. Walkways, again of discarded wooden ammo crates, connected one hooch to its neighbor, and provided a walkway to the "outdoor facilities" and showers.

The end of an extremely exhausting day seemed in sight. However, as we passed a sign directing us toward the Officers Club, Pete insisted that we stop for a beer or two and perhaps a chance to meet some of the docs and nurses. As we neared the club, the scent of the ocean became stronger, and the sound of music and laughter grew louder.

Parking on a cliff overlooking the South China Sea, I could hear but not see the breaking waves below. I could, however, plainly make out the lights of the U.S.S. Repose, a U.S. Naval Hospital Ship presently providing neurosurgical and ophthalmology support, sitting about a mile off shore.

Inside, I met the "fastest scalpel in the whole of Vietnam," a general surgeon who had just completed a rare appendectomy in slightly under seven minutes, skin to skin. I chatted with several orthopedic surgeons, all frustrated with the numerous amputations they were obligated to perform. I also met the two nurse anesthetists with whom I'd also share the hooch. They, like everyone else, had just completed a shift that began and ended in the dark, and were simply unwinding.

Finally, social obligations fulfilled and a short walk from the club, our hooch. I remember little else that night other than sliding my body onto a paper-thin mattress and placing my head on a scrawny but delightful pillow. One down; three hundred and sixty-four to go.

Welcome to Vietnam

Twenty dollar military scrip

A row of hooches

One-Star "accommodations" with a view of the South China Sea

Operating room at the ready

Chapter Four

The Hooch

A hooch is a hooch, is a hooch. What in the world can you say about a hooch? Well, if I were a fly on the wall of a hooch for a year, oh, what tales I could tell!

Ours was typical, probably twenty-four feet square, and raised about a foot off the ground to allow the monsoon rains to flow beneath it rather than through it. There was wood flooring, a tin roof, and a solid wooden door at the front and back. Walls were wooden slats for about two or three feet above the floor, with screening from there to the roof. On the outside were plastic flaps that could be raised or lowered to cover the screening and keep out the rain.

Outside our front door was a dilapidated old sofa, from God knows where, on which to sunbathe or simply relax if one wanted to "get out of the house." Fifty feet from the back door stood an eight foot high sandbag bunker, which on the day I arrived, I was told was never used.

Each of us had our own little niche in the hooch. There was some type of homemade desk and chair in the corner at the head of your bed, the bed draped in mosquito netting, and a locker at the foot of the bed.

In the center of the room was a large wooden spool, the kind used to transport telephone cable. Empty, on its side, and circled by a few rickety stools, it now served as our "coffee table."

Hanging above the table was a hundred-watt bulb, its light reflected by a small green, metal shade. From an adapter above it were five or six extension cords, shooting out to every corner of the hooch and powering radios, floor model fans, and even a hot plate.

A large Styrofoam chest, once used to transport whole blood from the states, sat beside the table. Always filled with either dry ice, also used to ship the blood, or ice bought at the nearby PX, it was used to refrigerate soda, beer, or left-over C-rations.

C-rations were a relatively scarce commodity among us non-combatants. Used in the field, troops disliked them because of the weight they added to their packs, and the fact that they usually had to eat them cold, often in the rain. Given to the emergency room staff by wounded soldiers once they were admitted to the hospital, these pre-packaged GI meals could be found squirreled away in hooches all over the hospital compound.

We "connoisseurs" often preferred the spaghetti and meatball dinner to mess hall powdered eggs for breakfast, or even beef stew to the "mystery meat" being served at lunch. There were even small desserts that were included in the meal like cookies or canned peaches that could be saved for a late-night snack, and a three-pack of cigarettes, usually Camels, that could be either smoked or traded.

Water, like C-rations, was also highly valued. Its use was prioritized to patient bathing, surgical scrubs, washing instruments, and the like. There were no water lines into the hooches; the nearest spigot for even brushing your teeth was in the community shower. Never drunk in its natural form because of the chlorine taste from the disinfecting process, it had to be disguised in iced tea, or used in powdered milk or coffee. Staff showers were intentionally short, not only because of the frigid water temperature, but also because we understood that due to only sporadic water truck deliveries, misuse would only increase the frequency we did without.

Soda and beer, on the other hand, were readily available, and could be found stacked by the case under each man's bunk, with cans chilling in the chest. Though readily available, the selection was extremely limited. Beer, for example, did not include any of the top ten brands sold at home. Not even any in the top twenty, for that matter. And if you really didn't care about the taste, the best bargain, at $2.30, was a case of brownish cans simply labeled "BEER."

Because of the easy accessibility of beer, even with its dreadful flavor, "Happy Hours" could be found going on at any time in the hooch, day or night, rain or shine. They seemed more natural, more acceptable, at eight or nine o'clock at night, but it was not uncommon to find them going on at the same time of the morning. With few days off, and one day no different from any other, the end of a long shift was reason enough to celebrate.

Of course, where there's plenty of beer and a bunch of guys, there's always poker. Two or three nights a week you could find a friendly game of nickel, dime, quarter, "dealer's choice" in any of several hooches. On the average you could win or lose ten or fifteen bucks, have a few beers, and fall exhausted into bed. In most games no one ever went broke, and certainly never got rich, but there were exceptions. There were hooches in which there were "all-nighters," and at a dollar or two, or even five to simply ante, games could get quite pricey.

On the rare nights when there were no poker games, those men not working could be found standing in line at a chosen hooch for the much-anticipated, highly advertised "skin flicks." Most would have a six pack in one hand, a beach chair in the other, and a dollar in their pocket to help cover the cost of someone buying and shipping the film from the states.

The screen was an old sheet hanging from the door at one end of the hooch, while the projector sat on top an old bar stool at the other end. The hooch was a buzz of activity with loud chatter, beer cans being opened, and chairs being dragged across the floor as each man jockeyed for the best seat in the house.

Suddenly, 3 - 2 - 1 appeared on the screen, and for the next hour or so - complete silence! In fact, not only was a word not spoken, but not a pair of eyes wandered from the screen other than to search for an occasional replacement beer.

"Skin flicks" were kind of a good thing! True, they did start hormones flowing where they really didn't need to be, but they were a "normal" activity men shared, like playing golf, or watching football on

TV. Any pastime that gave rise to rubbing elbows, other than standing next to each other and hovering over a patient in the emergency room or surgery, just couldn't be all that bad.

✳✳✳✳✳✳

As one might expect, however, where there were men and women together anywhere, sex would never be limited just to the movies. 2nd Surg was no different!

Temptation was as close as the bar stool next to you at the Officers Club, or across the table at the mess hall. Married, single, kids or none, with partners thousand of miles and months away, nature often took its course, and interest often gave way to planning opportunity.

Whether spur of the moment or planned over time, choices of meeting places, however, were few and far between. With no motel just down the road, and the family car parked some 7,000 miles away, where and when became an amusing game of sorts for those undertaking any romantic rendezvous.

The beach was within walking distance, but everyone had the same idea. Lying on a blanket, cool breeze blowing, moonlight shining, and not another soul in sight? An impossible dream!

An empty operating room with its narrow yet padded bed, a vacant x-ray department with its cold hard table, a cramped supply room, or even a sandbagged bunker were all utilized, or so I was told, at one time or another. But the fear of the war suddenly starting up again at any moment always left those having such affairs apprehensive about the possibility of being interrupted.

"Your place or mine?" became not only a popular pick-up line, but also by far the most attractive alternative to any of the more risky meeting places on the compound. For the plan to work, however, there had to be a party at the Officers Club, and your hoochmates had to join forces!

Parties were no problem! There were parties for birthdays, parties for engagements, and parties for promotions. There were parties for someone going home the next day, Halloween parties in May, and parties simply because it was Tuesday.

Most important, parties at the club guaranteed that practically all of Officers Row would attend. With everyone eager to celebrate the occasion or share companionship, and with friends willing to stay the course, hooches would empty, providing the perfect circumstances for those seeking privacy.

With the party underway, the couple could slip away, quickly lower the outside rain flaps, and stealthily sneak into the darkened hooch. Dropping the flaps, in fact, was akin to hanging a "Do Not Disturb" sign on the front door, a request graciously honored by all in the community.

※※※※※※

It might seem the hooch functioned merely as a bar and a brothel, but nothing could be further from the truth. Yeah, an awful lot of beer was consumed, and folks occasionally cavorted with naked neighbors, but all extra-curricular activity had purpose.

Many used alcohol simply to get to sleep, and to help them stay asleep. Nightly "outgoing," nearby "incoming," and the constant roar of helicopters landing and taking off not a city block away often made it impossible even to doze off, let alone to sleep soundly. As far as the romantic interludes, simply put the attitude was, "boys will be boys."

Most time in the hooch, however, was spent performing mundane tasks meant simply to devour the hours and days left in country.

Reading was a favorite pastime; perusing magazines from the PX, newspapers sent from home, or even the ever-popular Stars and Stripes, "The American Soldiers' Newspaper," provided free by Uncle Sam on a daily basis.

Hometown newspapers reported on the burning of draft cards and

conscientious objectors fleeing to Canada. There were accounts of the
Marines at Khe Sanh reinforcing their bunkers a day after they were
pounded by over 1,300 North Vietnamese artillery shells, and details of
the fight for Hill 875 at Dak To, the bloodiest and most costly battle of
the war.

Meanwhile, just like the Stars and Stripes in war zones over the past
fifty years, the need to restrict the flow of information to the enemy
limited the paper's ability to report in-country military matters. There
were stories on international affairs, items of interest from home such as
winter storms and stock activity, and, of course, the ever-popular comics
and sports pages. Throughout the paper could be found whimsical
anecdotes centering around troops in the field. One such tale related
how a soldier's hip wound was minimized when the round first went
through a can of lima beans and ham C-rations.

We did have one radio station, and it was great! Whenever anyone
was in the hooch, the radio was on, and AFVN (Armed Forces,
Vietnam), with its 50,000 watts, could be heard crisp and clear, twenty-
four hours a day.

Influenced primarily by Adrian Cronauer, the disc jockey famous for
introducing "GOOOOOOOOOD MORNING VIETNAM!!!" on his
early morning show two years earlier, the station's format was for the
most part up tempo top 100, and popular music. There was a splash of
Country and Western, but usually middle-of-the-road music on "Dawn
Busters" from six to nine a.m.; lots of oldies on "Million Dollar Music"
from three to five p.m.; and much of what was selling at home on the
"Orient Express" from one to four in the morning. Even spot
announcements on giving a GI a lift or GI benefits sounded much like
commercials in the states.

AFVN's audience was a young one - eighteen, nineteen, and twenty
year-olds yanked from comfortable environments, and dropped into the
middle of the biggest culture shock of their lives. Whether sleeping
under the stars in the middle of the jungle, riding a river patrol boat, or
pounding a typewriter in an office, they, like us, all needed a touch of
home, and Armed Forces Radio, Saigon, provided just that.

As one might expect, the radio was automatically turned on as all returned from mail call each afternoon, hands and arms full of so called "Care Packages" and letters from home. Goodie packages would be opened immediately, shared if edible such as cookies, or stashed away if it was your favorite candy bar.

Then each man would retreat beneath the mosquito netting on his bunk, secretly sniff the envelopes for any trace of his wife or sweetheart, and read and reread each letter several times.

Letter writing was reserved for later in the evening when the song on the radio reminded you of that special someone, when you could almost feel her as you looked at her picture, and you could tiredly write and softly say, "Goodnight, my love." Needless to say, days without mail were a bitch!

******

With so many hours spent working , and sleeping when you could, there was little time or ambition to do laundry, shine boots, or even clean the hooch. Enter, "Mama-San."

I don't think we ever really knew her name. We just simply called her Mama-San. A frail old lady from a nearby village, she, along with thousands of other locals, had permission to work on the base. Like most older Vietnamese, she, too, had teeth blackened from chewing beetle-nut, and wore the typical peasant black "pajamas," conical straw hat, and sandals. The only English she knew was "Number one" when referring to something good as in when we gave her a cigarette, "Number ten" when meaning something bad or dirty like the floor of the hooch, and "Me no VC" when in a kidding manner we asked her if she were Vietcong.

For $3 a week and an occasional carton of cigarettes from each guy in the hooch, every few days Mama-San would make our beds, shine our boots, sweep the floor, and straighten up a bit. She'd also take our dirty laundry home with her and wash it (heaven knows where), and return it on her next trip, neatly folded, fatigues pressed. Somehow we always got our own stuff back, but missing one sock, each and every time.

******

I'm certain life in our hooch was like any other on Officers Row, and probably quite similar to the hundreds in country with only minor differences. We may have gambled more and drunk less than others, or maybe it was the other way around. Some had TV, where we had none. Some could listen to Hanoi Hanna. We could not.

Regardless of the differences or similarities, the hooch was our home for a year; our hoochmates our "family." We all lived in the same "house" with no indoor plumbing. We all ate sausage and "something" for breakfast four days a week. We all endured the bitterly cold nights during the monsoon season, and the malaria-ridden mosquitos when it was hot and dry.

Over time, we learned each others' likes and dislikes, annoyances, and peculiarities. With absolutely no privacy, there were no secrets, and we openly shared our pasts and our hopes for the future.

We never discussed religion, but we hotly debated this "limited" war versus bombing North Vietnam off the face of the map. Gradually, most realized we weren't and couldn't win this war despite the enemy body counts. We all agreed, however, that to maintain sanity, all we could do was to continue to help fix broken bodies, and count the days until we went home.

All factors considered, I suppose a fly on the wall of one hooch probably couldn't tell a fly in a hooch 300 miles away a lot he didn't already know. What he could tell him, however, was that each man in every hooch had learned more about himself in one short year than he had in all his lifetime. In that respect, I guess, a hooch is a hooch, is a hooch.

Chapter Five

The Back Room

I could have sworn it was noon! Suddenly I woke lying on a sheet and pillowcase saturated with sweat rolling off my chest and dripping from my brow. Bright sunlight was streaming through the hooch screening, while two or three mosquitos were eyeing what they thought was their next meal through the netting around my bed.

Actually it was 6 a.m., and the start of my first full day in country. Pete was dressed and quietly straightening his bed. My other hoochmates had obviously left for breakfast and work. Outside, the wooden walkways were filled with guys heading back and forth to either the shower tent or the three-seater. Comically, but understandably, attire included either a towel around the waist and a shaving kit in hand, or underwear and a magazine or newspaper under their arm.

The day for me was a freebie of sorts with no work, but a busy one, nonetheless. Morning would find me unpacking and setting up my little corner of the hooch, in-processing, and hitchhiking to the PX for soda, soap, and the like. Meandering about the compound, I located the laundry for towels and sheets, stopped in Central Supply and introduced myself, and peeked into the Emergency Room, here called Receiving, for my first glimpse of a "push" or mass casualty situation. An admission clerk told me that eighteen badly wounded GIs had arrived within the past half hour.

Lunch time found the mess hall practically empty with only a few stragglers lucky enough to have the day off or working the night shift. Those involved in the push, and unable to eat, however, were not forgotten. Food service personnel shuttled trays of sandwiches, soup, and drinks to the various departments of the hospital, apparently a task performed on a regular basis.

By mid-afternoon I was meeting with the Chief Nurse and being told my fate. I learned there was a tremendous enemy buildup in the area, and the hospital was overstaffing with emergency room and operating room nurses to meet the expected demands. Presently, however, we had far too many operating room nurses, and too few emergency room nurses. So, being the new kid on the block I was elected to cross train in Receiving, and would be assigned to the operating room as those nurses rotated home, and new emergency room nurses arrived. Willingly, almost gladly, I accepted the opportunity to broaden my knowledge, and to get that front row seat of the war for which I was so eager.

Pete was to be my mentor, and I was advised to imitate his every move. However, my first lesson in combat nursing began then and there in the office of the Chief Nurse. Nursing in 'Nam, I was told, was all about caring and proficiency. "Without caring, you're useless to your patients, and without proficiency you jeopardize lives," still rings in my ears today.

Caring, I was told, was more than simply going through the motions of trying to meet a patient's needs. "Here's a blanket to get warm," or "Are you married?" were probably empty words to a man looking for some much needed compassion. Touching his shivering arm as you put the blanket over him, on the other hand, would tell him you knew he was chilled to the bone. Asking his wife's name or if he had kids meant you were concerned about him as a husband and a father, and not just making idle conversation.

Being proficient meant being not only good or very good, but almost perfect in those skills needed by every nurse in Receiving. Would I be confident enough to call out a blood pressure of fifty over forty without re-inflating the cuff to reassure myself of what I heard? Could I insert a peripheral IV catheter every time on patients often in shock and with veins getting smaller by the minute? The answer had to be "Yes," or my "internship" would be a short one. The question was, however, how could I gain such experience if not under actual conditions? Fear not. There was an answer!

Whether two, ten, or twenty casualties came through the Receiving front door, the triage officer literally had his hands full. A surgeon himself, he would assist in the treatment of the casualties, but at the same time had the sole responsibility of prioritizing care according to the patient's needs, and the availability of surgeons and operating rooms, including staff. If delaying treatment put a life at risk, that patient merited immediate care. If, on the other hand, a soldier had a minor wound, and was in no immediate danger, treatment could be deferred until the urgent needs of others were met.

It must be emphasized that the philosophy of triage is to do the greatest good for the greatest numbers. Not infrequently, a decision by the triage officer hinged on the possible hopelessness of treatment. Attempting to save an individual who had little or no chance of survival, while depleting blood supplies and consuming large numbers of staff, would serve only to endanger patients who might otherwise weather the storm of serious injury using the same resources.

When the gut-wrenching decision had to be made to cease resuscitative efforts on individuals who could not be saved, civilian or soldier, American or Vietnamese, he or she would be moved from the mainstream of casualties. Quietly, quickly, respectfully, the patient would be moved to the so called "Back Room," a holding area to the rear of the department, while the all-out life-saving effort continued in the receiving area.

Here, patients were made comfortable, a nurse constantly at their side as their lives slowly slipped away. Here, I learned, is where I would spend my first few days of orientation to Receiving, and here, I was told I would come to understand "caring," and would gain some expertise in skills that would be expected of me at the same time.

My first day in the back room lasted fourteen hours. I thought Pete was testing my stamina a bit that day, but I found there would be many more just like it. We began at 7 a.m., and I was assigned to care for two North Vietnamese soldiers, both victims of multiple gunshot wounds. I had yet to meet a Vietnamese let alone the enemy, and never in my young nursing career sat with a patient I knew for certain would die on my watch.

The hours were filled with taking and recording blood pressures, and observing alterations in respiratory effort. Emotions, whatever they were, were channeled into keeping busy, walking between patients and observing each. I had no idea how to feel or how I felt toward these men, and agonized over the possible inappropriateness of my lack of sensitivity.

My saving grace that day was that Pete spent many hours with me between his duties in receiving. We toured the entire department, including the receiving area, with discussions on what my duties would eventually include. We noted paperwork and supplies and the need to conserve the latter. He focused his attention, however, on a primary reason I was assigned to the back room: to master starting IVs.

******

Hemorrhage from battle wounds, big or small, results in diminished blood volume, which can quickly lead to hypovolemic shock. The most urgent need of casualties arriving at 2nd Surg, therefore, was volume replacement.

The instant a stretcher hit the sawhorses in Receiving, a nurse would be at the side of the patient, introducing themselves, grabbing an arm, applying a tourniquet, and looking for a vein in which to place a large gauge intravenous catheter. Never easy, the task was often more difficult because veins were even smaller due to dehydration brought on by spending days in the jungle.

With time being the enemy of the soldier and the trauma teams, and the need to maintain the integrity of all infusion sites, "amateurs"were strictly forbidden from trying to start IVs. Opportunities for beginners such as me to gain experience, however, lay within the department in the form of dying Vietnamese to whom I was assigned. They were small of stature with small veins that were probably now collapsing. Theory was that if I could repeatedly start an IV on these patients, I would most certainly be able to "stick" GIs on a regular basis. The practice, never allowed on American soldiers, was in no way meant to dehumanize these patients, but rather seen as an aid in ensuring the survival of those under our care in the days to come.

With the many hours spent in the back room, I soon became very good at starting IVs. At the same time, emotions began bubbling to the surface in varying degrees, ranging from pure indifference to almost outright grief, and I knew that the "caring" required of me was well within my reach.

As I watched the broken and bleeding bodies of young Americans arrive in Receiving, I began to curse the uniform of the North Vietnamese soldiers. I thought nothing of their families until coming across pictures in their gear. I thought nothing of their country until claiming coins falling from their pockets onto the stretcher on which they laid. I curiously eyed their jet black hair, their lack of a beard, and their calloused trigger fingers. I acknowledged to myself, however, that they were in fact men losing their lives.

Fair-skinned and sunburned, not yet tanned from weeks or months in country, is how I remembered most American kids I cared for in the back room. Short, tall, skinny, muscles from head to toe, black, white, and native American, all were semiconscious or unconscious, and within hours if not minutes of dying.

Going through their wallets and gear to aid in positively identifying the soldier opened a Pandora's box into his life, and these moments troubled me. A driver's license told me where he lived, often making him a neighbor. A girl's picture and no pictures of kids told me this was his girlfriend, and not a wife. A fake ID proving him to be twenty-one indicated that he, like thousands of other kids, had beaten the system to have those few manly drinks before leaving home.

Stretchers in the back room were laid directly on the floor rather than on sawhorses. More often than not, I sat on a small wooden stool to one side of the patient, holding his hand on that side between the two of mine. There was little else I could do other than touch and talk, but I assumed that to be the best medicine at the time, and gave it in large doses.

Assuming they could hear, perhaps even comprehend, I always talked to the soldiers under my care. During such chitchats, probably more for my sake than theirs, I thought they needed to know I was there, that I would do all I could to keep them comfortable.

I gave men in obvious pain medication in doses sufficient not to simply reduce, but to eliminate their suffering. When I thought there was a need, I comforted men with a moist cloth to their forehead, face, or chest. Occasionally I cooled them by using a newspaper as a fan.

As the hours passed, however, sometimes quietly, more often abruptly, signs of pending death would begin to appear. Gurgling respirations or deep inhalations followed by long periods of non-breathing; rapid, weak, irregular pulses; and rapidly falling blood pressures terrified me.

When pulses were finally absent and respirations had ceased, I would summon a physician to pronounce the patient dead, and notify Graves Registration to transfer the body. I gathered and bagged personal belongings, completed and attached body tags, and more often than not, gave a long solemn stare at the man's face with a thousand and one thoughts running through my mind as to who he was and why he had died.

I had given my all, physically and emotionally, to men that I knew were about to die, and who in all likelihood, never knew I had stood by their side. I had talked to each, heard their voices in my head, and had come to know them. I had briefly peered into their lives, looking at photos of families who would soon bury them, and felt the pain they were sure to endure. I had cared for them, and I had cared about them.

Finally, the time would arrive to transport the body. Zipping the body bag closed, symbolically at least, removed the man's face from my memory; as did sending his record along, his name. Verifying with Graves Registration that in fact the body was that of "Private Jones" or "Corporal Smith" assigned responsibility for the individual to the U.S. Army, and cut whatever emotional ties that might have developed over the past many hours.

******

By the end of my stretch in the back room I was able to thread an IV catheter on any of my petite Vietnamese patients on my first attempt every time. I was confident I could do the same on any wounded American soldier.

I also felt that I had brought with me the ability to care deeply for my patients, and the ability to convey that message to them. Each would know that my concern was for the man inside the bloody, mud-caked uniform demonstrated with a query as to a nickname, a gentle touch on the shoulder, or simply wiping away a tear rolling down his cheek.

I had "graduated," and would soon be brought to the main receiving room for a few days of orientation, and finally assigned as staff. Though I yearned to get to the operating room, I eagerly anticipated what might prove to be an experience of a lifetime.

C-Rations and a Smoke

2nd Surg Chapel

A break from the action with Stars and Stripes

Outgoing artillery

Chapter Six

By The Numbers

I suppose some muckamucks in Washington decided that one way to keep Americans abreast of our efforts in the war was, on a regular basis, to provide numbers substantiating our winning ways. After all, when a person sees, for example, a half-time basketball score of 66-28, the person can make an assumption of the outcome with fairly strong confidence.

Newspapers sent from home were replete with body counts, body counts, and more body counts. Even the Stars and Stripes, in two separate articles, informed readers that 329 communists were killed around landing zones recently, 32 enemy were killed by the 196th Light Infantry Brigade near Tam Ky, that the Americal Division accounted for 72 enemy kills in several firefights, 15 more Vietcong were killed during a charge on an outpost, and finally 37 enemy were killed during search and destroy missions. In one commentary, there was mention of four Americans killed, but otherwise no further references to injuries or casualties.

******

It was now mid-January of 1968, and we had lost some 11,000 young Americans the year before; the South Vietnamese over 12,000 of their own. The North Vietnamese had sacrificed 134,000 lives during the same period. It seemed pure and simple we were winning the war militarily, but the same newspapers from home were reporting on draft dodgers and anti-war demonstrations. All reasons, of course, for hot debate on those nippy monsoon evenings in our home away from home.

On the other hand, discussions were a lot less heated when Dust-Off pilots joined in for an evening of imbibing at the Officers Club. We nurses tended to simply listen, to allow the fly-boys to vent, to talk, often with a quiver in their voices, about the events of their day. Theirs was a scary occupation, often filled with harrowing moments. Reliving the experience one more time seemed to help them put it all behind them.

To say that flying Dust-Off, especially in this part of the country, was dangerous, would be a gross understatement. First, helicopter crew members accounted for 10% of all those killed in Vietnam. Second, over 215 helicopters of all types had been shot down in the past six months. Last, there were 44 provinces in South Vietnam. Enemy activity was the heaviest in four of the northernmost provinces. As a result, it was in these provinces that over 50% of all American soldiers killed during the war died. The territory or Dust-Off pilots covered? You guessed it, these same four provinces and several more.

Pilots always had the option of declining missions because of darkness, weather, or enemy activity around the landing zones, but there was never a shortage of crews willing to roll the dice because of the urgent needs of the wounded. As a result, those aviators paid the price dearly. Of the 1,400 Dust-Off pilots in country, 40 were killed in 1967 by hostile fire; 48 died from night and inclement weather crashes; and another 380 were wounded, totaling a full one-third of their group's numbers being injured or killed.

Tricks to beat the odds came in many shapes and forms. High-speed, tight-circle approaches were the norm for all landings, but regardless, in one of every 300 missions, their aircraft was hit by enemy fire. Many crew members wore additional armor known as "chicken plates," on their chests and backs, to protect against rounds coming through the front glass cockpit or the open side door to their rear. Occasionally, they even sat on their steel helmet to provide additional "butt armor."

Whether bold or conservative in their choices of missions, these guys deserved our admiration. With over 56,000 wounded in action in 1967, and only 116 Medical Evacuation Helicopters in country, their days were long, their missions frequent, and none were normal.

******

To get off the subjects of flying and dying, we often tapped our aviator friends for news found on the in-country grapevine. Some tidbits were most often released weeks or months after the fact, while others never became common knowledge. However, changing the tone of the conversation was usually next to impossible.

We knew, for example, that two nurses had died in a freak helicopter crash near Saigon in 1966, but on a dreary December night in 1967 learned that four Army nurses had been killed in an aircraft mishap near Qui Nhon. All were returning to their units when the plane went into the side of a mountain in inclement weather. They were friends to some and comrades to all, and the news of their deaths was unnerving.

Our tree of invincibility was again shaken when, a few months later, pilots told us of assaults on the 3rd Surgical Hospital in the south near Dong Tam. Frequent mortar attacks, thirteen in all, had resulted in hits on the lab, x-ray, and other buildings, including the nurses' quarters. It seemed that the war was indeed heating up, and Quonset huts with red crosses on top no longer mattered to Charlie and friends.

******

Occasionally officers from surrounding combat units would also visit the Officers Club for a bit of socializing. In addition to relaxing conversation and news from home, we'd also hear details of events usually kept within units, seldom reported very far up the chain of command, and certainly never publicized. Incidents swept under the rug included drug use, suicides, friendly fire casualties, and a deadly pastime among the troops known as "fragging."

Fragging was just a nice wartime term for homicide. Fifty, sixty, or seventy times a year (no one knows for sure), grunts, fearful that the combat tactics of young and inexperienced sergeants and officers would get them killed, would decide to take matters into their own hands. By rolling a fragmentation, or frag grenade, into the sleeping quarters of the commanders they resented in the middle of the night, perceptions were the odds of their own survival increased dramatically and instantly. Victims of these crimes, like those in the two previous wars, never survived, and likewise, the perpetrators never identified.

Friendly fire casualty statistics, on the other hand, were a bit more accurate, and as one might expect, rose proportionately each year as the number of troops increased. Slowly the numbers grew in 1966 from about 200 men a month to 450 a month in 1967. In early 1968, over 500 men a month were dying from such mishaps, and though deaths were predictable, little could be done to reduce them.

******

Shooting the breeze with other soldiers while shopping or standing in line at the PX, or chitchatting while waiting your turn at the barber shop, would give anyone a good feel for the amount of drug use in country. Sniffing the night air while strolling the hospital compound most nights would, likewise, validate any preconceived notions. Marijuana, heroin, opiates, and other drugs were readily available, less adulterated than at home, dirt cheap, and widely used in Vietnam.

There was an unwritten law that forbade soldiers from using drugs in the field for the fear of the consequences of enemy detection. So serious was an infraction of this rule, that violators were usually beaten to within an inch of their lives when detected, and a second incident usually avoided with the subtle threat of fragging.

Meanwhile, at bases and camps from Da Nang to the Delta, with over 50% of grunts lighting up bongs or marijuana pipes, and 10 to 15% using razor blades and miniature spoons, it's a small wonder that our troops even showed up to fight the war.

Drugs also played a minor part in the 40 or so reported suicides each year during the war. Mellowed out on a barbiturate, and tortured by the fears of battle or even the silence of the nighttime jungle, some men choose to end their suffering by simply placing the barrel of an M16 between their eyes, and somehow managing to pull the trigger. Most died instantly, while a few spent the last hours of their lives in the back room at 2nd Surg or other hospitals. Actual numbers of suicides may well have been much higher, since superiors and even medical facilities often listed these men as killed in action rather than have families or units bear the stigma of suicide.

✳✳✳✳✳✳

There are thousands of other statistics available that demonstrate both the inhumanity and scope of the conflict. As an example, as troop deployment increased, the lone hospital in Nha Trang in 1962 became two dozen by 1967, and a handful of nurses grew to over 800.

Almost 5,300 beds in country were kept at about 60% occupancy with medical patients, surprisingly, rather than surgical patients, accounting for five out of six admissions. Cumulatively, such admissions were the greatest drain on American troop strength during the entire war.

Some problems, such as diarrheal and skin conditions, kept large numbers of men off the battlefield for just a few days, while others, such as hepatitis, kept a few out of action for much longer periods of time.

Fears of the plague, thankfully, never materialized. However, as expected, malaria was the most significant medical problem of the war. On average, about 8,000 soldiers a year contracted the disease, each requiring up to twenty days hospitalization.

✳✳✳✳✳✳

Battle casualties, on the other hand, though the smaller number of admissions, required much longer periods of hospitalization, utilized more supplies, and demanded a greater number of staff.

In the operating rooms of 2nd Surg, surgery was performed on between 300 and 400 patients a month. Of these men 60% were classified as "major" with 3 or 4 major wounds, 25% as "moderate" with 2 or 3 major wounds, and the remaining 15% "minor."

Major wounds necessitated "cracking a chest," or a thoracotomy, "opening a belly" or an exploratory laparotomy, craniotomy, major facial reconstruction, vascular or ocular repairs, or amputations.

Fragmentation wounds requiring tissue debridement, no matter how extensive, were usually considered minor.

Of the 350 or so men having surgery at 2nd Surg each month, 25% would eventually be classified as severely disabled; a third of those, totally disabled. Approximately five of the 350 would have limbs amputated, and half of these men would have multiple limbs removed.

Amputations were 300% more likely than in previous wars because of the enemy's ability to hide mines and trip wires to booby traps in the dense foliage. Likewise, a single gunshot was often more lethal because of the newer high-velocity weapons. However, there were far fewer American deaths per man wounded than in either the Korean conflict or World War Two, and many factors contributed to such a meaningful decline.

With a dozen Dust-Off detachments strategically placed throughout the country, wounded on the battlefield were guaranteed a rapid response, and often following an heroic extraction, usually less than a thirty - minute flight to the nearest hospital.

The availability of thousands upon thousand of units of whole blood or fresh frozen plasma, kept at temperature in Styrofoam chests destined to someday become hooch refrigerators, undoubtedly contributed to reduced mortality. While there were some type-specific units of blood available, the greater majority were O positive, or the universal donor, able to be used on any patient. Eliminating the time necessary for typing and cross matching each unit of blood aided greatly in avoiding or reversing the effects of shock upon many patients.

Well-equipped hospitals managed by competent, able administrators, likewise, increased the odds of the survival for troops. However, the entire story of patient survival - like that of chopper pilots who occasionally guzzled beer, but always flew by the seat of their pants, or grunts who sometimes smoked pot, but always fought valiantly - can't be told entirely with statistics. A closer look at the training of nurses and physicians in the idiosyncrasies of combat medicine, and a peek into the rooms in which these patients were cared for may give a hint as to why many of these men walked the earth in 1969 when seriously wounded in 1968. A walk through receiving or the operating rooms might indeed explain why this war was more than simply just a matter of numbers.

Chapter Seven

The Main Room

It was an eerie feeling, almost surreal, as Pete and I approached the main room of Receiving on my first day as staff. The outside walls were lined with drying upright stretchers, a night rain having washed the blood from their canvas into the mud below.

Inside, a freshly mopped floor, not yet dry because of the oppressive humidity, was stamped with the footprints of men hastening about to replace supplies used during the night. Bottles of lactated Ringers solutions were being hung; IV supplies replenished; and rolls of tape strategically placed. Finally, sawhorses were being aligned with exactness to await the next incoming litters.

In the next hour or so the hospital around us awakened quickly. Nurses and corpsmen in Central Supply began folding linen to make packs, firing up the gasoline-heated sterilizers, and delivering supplies to the wards. There, men wounded and operated on one or two days earlier were being prepared for evacuation to larger hospitals for further treatment and rehabilitation. Lab techs were examining blood drawn from soldiers who had straggled in during the night complaining of chills and fever, while admission clerks were preparing their charts - diagnosis: possible fulciform malaria.

Suddenly a radioman entered Receiving to announce "Dust-Off, five minutes from the hospital with ten souls on board, four on litters, six ambulatory." I shadowed Pete as he called the triage physician and other surgeons on call for the day. Alerted also were the lab, x-ray, the operating room, and admissions.

My heart was in my throat as we stood in the doorway, watching the helicopter softly glide to a landing. I knew that what we were about to see would not be a pretty sight. These men were members of an early morning patrol who fell prey to a booby trap laid by the Vietcong during the night.

The pace swung into high gear as the corpsmen aboard the helicopter directed the litter bearers to carry the most seriously injured soldier to Receiving first. The remaining three litter patients followed within seconds, their litters, too, being carefully placed on the sawhorses. The litter bearers then returned to the helicopter to assist the ambulatory patients on board.

The first patient had obviously stepped directly on the mine. His left leg had been blown away at the knee, leaving a tattered, charred, bloody stump. His right leg was riddled with fragments and bleeding profusely.

Immediately, the patient was surrounded by a team acting in unison-corpsmen cutting away clothing, while a physician examined the wounds and aided in applying bilateral tourniquets. A nurse started an IV as a clerk asked the necessary questions for admission papers. "Do you want your family notified?" "No," came the trembling reply. All worked feverishly to prevent the patient from slipping further into shock. Another IV is started and the flow of Ringers solution opened wide.

The other men received similar care. The exploding mine had sprayed fragments into all parts of their bodies, tearing major vessels, splintering bones, and puncturing lungs. All their immediate needs were met; airways maintained, hemorrhage suppressed, fractured limbs splinted, chest wounds sealed, and chest tubes inserted.

******

The triage officer, who had briefly examined each patient and directed their initial care, met briefly with the operating room supervisor, and directed that three of the four operating rooms be opened immediately. One room would receive the patient who had stepped on the mine within the next fifteen or twenty minutes. The remaining two would receive other seriously injured patients directly from x-ray. His decision was based primarily on the condition of the patients, but also on the availability of specialty surgeons, the number of operating room personnel available, and the total number of patients who would require surgery. The decision to open the remaining room would be made after evaluating the surgical needs of the remaining patients more fully.

The operating room supervisor then returned to her department, and assigned personnel to set up rooms according to the following schedule:

Room	Patient	Surgeons	Procedures
1	Sgt. A	Vascular/General Orthopedic	Right femoral artery repair; left above the knee amputation; exploratory laparotomy; possible liver resection; debridement of legs & abdomen.
2	Pvt. B	Ophthalmology Neurosurgery General	Enucleation left eye; craniotomy; exploratory laparotomy; possible bowel resection; debridement of all extremities.
3	Lt. C	Thoracic/General Vascular	Left axillary artery repair; right thoracotomy & possible lung resection; laparotomy with spleenectomy; debridement of all extremities.

The triage officer now divided his time among assigning surgeons to the operating rooms, reading x-rays, and aiding in the care of the remaining patients. These men, fortunately, were some distance from the exploding mine, and x-rays and physical findings ruled out the need for immediate surgery. Each man would, however, require debridement of his many fragment wounds.

The operating room supervisor and triage officer again met briefly. They agreed that, since these patients were in no immediate danger, all operating room personnel would first assist in opening the three multiple procedure rooms, and that in approximately half an hour, when conditions had somewhat stabilized, the additional room would be opened to avoid lengthy delays for the remaining patients. These men, therefore, would be returned to Receiving following x-rays, have their wounds shaved if easily accessible and not extremely painful, and have IV fluids begun.

Within two hours another helicopter was announced and arrived with three men on board. While patrolling through dense jungle, the fire pin of a grenade attached to the flak jacket worn by one of the men, caught on thick foliage, separated from the grenade, and fell to the ground. Two of the three man patrol were able to react, turn, and begin to run from the device as it exploded. The young man carrying the grenade had no opportunity to free himself from the armament.

The two men able to respond to the danger were fortunately wearing flak jackets and steel helmets. They received only minor multiple fragment wounds of the extremities. The soldier caught in the middle of this unfortunate accident, however, was deemed "expectant," and transferred to the back room.

Another hour passed, and another helicopter touched down. By this time of the day, encounters with the enemy had begun to occur, and wound types shifted from the mutilation caused by mine fragments to the havoc brought on by small arms fire. High-velocity rounds often left small entrance wounds, but huge exit wounds with massive damage in between. With its tremendous kinetic energy, tumbling and even disintegration of its jacket, a bullet passing through the abdomen or chest not only shredded vital organs through which it passed, but tended to thrombus veins and arteries far from its path.

Noon became one o'clock, then two, then three. The patients kept coming! Another quadriplegic; another attempted suicide; another self-inflicted wound, done to escape the horror of the battlefield. Hour after hour, one helicopter after the other; the carnage seemed never to cease.

Day became evening, and the type of wounds again changed with the setting of the sun. Fire fights had ended with the darkness, but Charlie seemed destined to continue the struggle with mortar attacks into any base camp he could find. Multiple fragment wounds, again on this night, beat out bullet wounds as top contender for honors in the category of causing the most casualties.

******

Amidst all this horror, however, there were a few light-hearted moments, but unfortunately for him, at the expense of a North Vietnamese soldier. Wounded in both legs, he was captured after a fierce fire fight. Being the equivalent of a Captain in our Army, he was felt to be a possible valuable source of enemy troop movement information. An interpreter was summoned and questioning begun, while medics dressed his wounds and started an intravenous.

Once he arrived at 2nd Surg, he was examined, x-rayed, and placed on the surgical schedule for debridement of the gunshot wounds of both thighs, and insertion of a pin in one leg to provide skeletal traction as treatment of a fractured femur in that leg. All the while the questioning continued, but apparently with little success.

With the patient about to go to surgery, and frustration mounting, interrogators asked if I cared to play a role in a "good cop, bad cop" scheme to speed up the process. I'd have no lines, but was told my "acting" could well turn the tide. Seemed like a good way to break up a lousy day, and at the same time help the good guys, so I naturally volunteered, and like a kid in his first school play, nervously took my position as directed at the side of the patient.

"Fiddle with his IV tubing a bit," an American MP told me. "Wrap it around your finger a few times. Kink it once in a while." I did as suggested.

Meanwhile, a Vietnamese interpreter renewed the conversation, and suddenly the patient's eyes began bouncing between looking at my eyes, those of the interpreter, and my hands. Seems he was being told that the intravenous fluid he was receiving was keeping him alive, the implication being that if the flow was interrupted, he might well be joining his ancestors in the land of Buddha. Superstitious to begin with and unsure of the scruples of those gathered 'round, the patient's uneasiness became apparent with his squirming on the stretcher. Again, however, meaningful information was not to be had.

A few knock-knock jokes with the inevitable ha-has that followed went back and forth to give the patient the idea we were enjoying what we were doing, but now it was time for the interrogators to play their trump card.

"Now take your scissors from your chest pocket," I was told. "Open and close them a few times, real close to the IV tubing, and then look Charlie in the eye and smile."

Fidgeting soon became panic, and though I spoke not a word of Vietnamese, I could surely understand the sound of this man begging for his life. Calmly the Vietnamese interpreter reached up, and gently pushed my hand away from the IV tubing, as he again began to speak softly to the patient. He thanked me for his assistance, and told me I could leave, and as I slowly backed away, I could see the terror in the eyes of the wounded soldier. Needless to say, the guy talked until he was blue in the face, and the good guys got information useful to their cause!

The silliness lasted only a short while, and after a short smoke break, it was back to reality with the announcement of more incoming choppers and patients. Pockets were refilled with intravenous catheters, bottles of IV solutions hung, tubings connected and filled, blood mopped from the floor, and sawhorses were aligned. Soon the room was again filled with the broken bodies of youthful GIs.

Within minutes, used tracheostomy trays, cut-down trays, and chest tube trays littered the sides of the room. Kick buckets were filling with empty IV bottles, blood bags, and bloody gauze, and the floor beneath stretchers was strewn with bloody boots, uniforms, and gear.

Some soldiers were being wheeled directly to the operating rooms with lacerated livers, eviscerated bowels, or a severed carotid artery. Others stopped off at x-ray with fractures, facial trauma, or spinal cord injuries. Some men were being told they would lose a limb, were paralyzed from the waist down, or would lose the sight in one eye. One man was informed that the shrapnel in his back might necessitate the removal of one of his kidneys, while another was told the rusty fragments in his forearm had severed the nerves to his hand, making it useless. Another man probably couldn't hear a word because of his severe head trauma. On and on, the misery seemed to never end.

With their usual punctuality, the night shift arrived at 7 p.m., and after a short verbal report, they spread out across the room to aid the patients most in need of their care. Though grubby and extremely tired, not one nurse or corpsman on the day shift ever thought about leaving over the next few hours it took to get patients to the operating room, and to stabilize and prepare those who were required to wait.

******

That first day did end, of course, and with blood dried on our boots and caked beneath our finger nails, we headed straight for the Officers Club. This was an everyday tradition, especially among male nurses, that had been going on ever since 2nd Surg had opened its doors. We called it the Journal Club for lack of a better name, but it was more an excuse to have a few beers, and a chance to unwind before hitting the ice cold showers. More important, it was an opportunity to informally hash over what had been learned in "Combat Nursing 101" over the past 12 or 13 hours.

At the club meeting following my first day as staff, I was told that it was quite acceptable for a novice such as myself to await instruction and ask for assistance. I was also told my beginner status would be a thing of the past within a matter of days. "This time next week" I'd be expected to anticipate the need for and start a second IV, apply tourniquets, and acquire and prepare special trays without being told to do so. The learning curve, I would find, would be a steep one with little time for pampering.

Another issue discussed at this first meeting was the fact that some of the guys felt that the faces coming through the front door all seemed to be the same sunburned, mud-covered kid from Iowa, only with different injuries. It was a cold reminder that these were men on stretchers in front of us, not simply "multiple fragment wounds," and that perhaps we might consider looking into the eyes of our patients a bit more often.

With patients arriving at a frenzied pace, my second day was similar to the first, and days after that, much like the day before. Clinically, I was gaining a world of knowledge, but the skills that I discovered would serve me best were listening and prioritizing.

Weeding out the conversations or comments from those folks surrounding a patient never seemed to be a problem. Having worked as an operating room nurse, I was used to listening to the surgeon and assistant discussing their stock options, while the anesthesiologist was ordering lunch over the intercom with the secretary at the front desk, and the scrub tech at the same time was asking for additional suture.

Listening and filtering out the important tidbits also helped me develop a knack for prioritizing responses during these surgeries. On an open cholecystectomy (gallbladder removal), for example, a physician might mutter that he'd probably explore the common bile duct for a gallstone, and that he'd probably also perform an incidental appendectomy. Surgical etiquette, if you will, dictates an appendectomy be performed last because of the small chance of contaminating the abdominal cavity with bowel spillage from the appendix. Common sense, therefore, calls for supplying the scrub tech with the instruments for exploring the common bile duct before the phenol solution to cauterize the appendix stump.

This, however, was a far cry from such a cozy environment, and caring for a patient with relatively a relatively minor problem. Deciding whether to nonchalantly provide a forceps or phenol versus now all of a sudden, prioritizing between an intubation tube and an intravenous, would be like comparing soup to steak. Dealing with the agony these men were enduring, learning the basics of triage, reacting with the level of skill required, and doing so as if on a pair of roller skates were monumental tasks.

I'd leave Receiving appreciating the need for the skills and dedication of emergency room nurses. I thoroughly understood the challenges they faced, and had a better feel for those I would surely encounter in the operating room. I had learned that the willingness to act with confidence in abilities brought with me and learned alongside Pete were an integral part of a team acting in unison to increase the odds of young men's survival. I also realized that the same eagerness would serve well the patients I would care for in the days to come.

From my first day in the back room to my last hour in Receiving, though coming to detest the men who mutilated them, I had come to truly care for my patients. I had, for their sakes, become remarkably proficient. It was time to put into practice what I had learned, now in rooms where the painful moans would be silenced by anesthesia while the fight for life and limb continued.

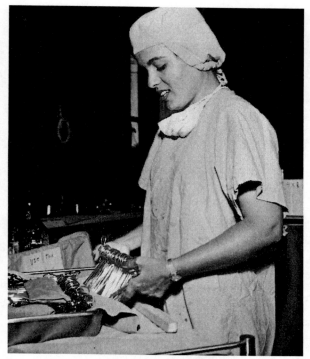

Instrument assembly in Central Supply

Dust-Off unloading patients

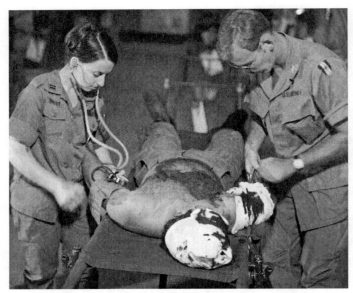

Receiving nurses caring for a casualty

Triage in receiving

Chapter Eight

The People You Meet

I remember few faces of those I met in 'Nam and even fewer names. Some I recall simply because of the spectacular impression they left in my mind; others for what they represented; and still others for the emotions they stirred in me about how right, or wrong, or rotten this war really was.

I can still picture the "fastest scalpel in the whole of Vietnam" as a little guy, probably about 5' 6" tall and 90 pounds soaking wet. He truly regarded those under his knife as men, not merely as a "multiple fragment debridement" or an "exploratory laparotomy." He was a great "meatball" surgeon with the speed and skill to save lives and salvage limbs.

One of the orthopedic surgeons, on the other hand, was a big man, well over 6' 2" and weighing over 200 pounds. He had huge hands, and I can still see him applying dressings to below-the-knee amputations day after day.

People who made the biggest impression on me, however, were from outside the hospital, from different parts of Vietnam, different cultures, and even from different parts of the world.

******

One of the most "colorful characters" I met was a wounded Republic of Korea, or ROK, soldier. Shot in the lower back by a hiding VC, he refused treatment and evacuation until he had first tracked down and killed his attacker.

When he arrived at 2nd Surg, he was still wearing the same bright orange scarf around his neck worn by many ROK soldiers in the jungle. He explained it helped the enemy in finding them in the dense foliage, but at the same time sent the message that any fight they started, they were bound to lose in dramatic fashion. Fierce fighters all, the ROKs seldom took prisoners.

Many different uniforms came through our front doors, of course. Some friendly; some not so friendly.

About one in fifty patients were South Vietnamese, members of the Army of the Republic of Vietnam, or ARVN soldiers. They in fact had their own ARVN hospitals to which they were normally evacuated, but the few men we did see appeared to be tough, scrappy fighters.

Occasionally we'd get a North Vietnamese or Vietcong POW from a nearby prison camp in for treatment, escorted by two of the burliest MPs you'd ever seen. They'd walk him in, hands cuffed behind his back, and not-so-gently lift him onto a stretcher.

Through an interpreter the prisoner would usually complain of excruciating abdominal pain that had begun only hours before. His blood pressure was usually low and falling, and his pulse fast and thready. His abdomen would be as rigid as a board.

He would usually insist that no incident had prompted the pain, except perhaps his slipping on a bar of soap in the shower and falling several days ago. Welts on his abdomen, flanks, and back would tell a different story.

With a preliminary diagnosis of blunt force trauma, Receiving staff would immediately and collectively move toward preparing the patient for immediate surgery. He would be stripped of his prison uniform. Staff then would take blood for a hematocrit and hemoglobin measurement, and do a quick shave prep of his abdomen. Two intravenous lines would be started. On one, a unit of O positive blood would be hung. Within minutes the gurney on which he lay would be en route to the operating room.

Every time - not eight or nine times out of ten, but every time, - the exploratory abdominal surgery done to diagnose and treat the problem would reveal any one of a number of blunt trauma injuries. A short list might include capsular tears of the liver, pancreatic lacerations, spleenic ruptures, kidney contusions, and even mesenteric (arteries providing blood to the bowel) damage.

The MPs who brought the patient would now be long gone, having done their duty by simply bringing the patient to the hospital. Having seen similar situations, they knew the cause and effect of the man's injuries. Perhaps they were the result of an extremely brutal interrogation or an angry response to his actions towards his captors. Regardless, they considered the injuries to be the price you pay for being the enemy. Receiving staff, while not condoning the behavior, understood.

※※※※※※

North Vietnamese "regulars" and Vietcong would also occasionally arrive at 2nd Surg as fresh battlefield casualties, now captives of U.S. forces. These patients, like any others, received prompt and professional care, but the interrogation begun on the battlefield and continued on the Dust-Off flight often became its most intense just as the patient's condition was being evaluated. Knowledge gained from these men regarding their unit size and destination would frequently lead to redeployment of troops or creation of new "search and destroy" missions. Military police and interrogators were not about to allow such vital information simply to roll off with the patient to the operating room.

The arrival of North Vietnamese or Vietcong, of course, always caused an uproar in Receiving. Within minutes the grapevine would have brought lab techs, x-ray techs, nurses, and corpsmen scurrying from all corners of the hospital to get a glimpse of Charlie.

Vietcong tended to be frightened teenagers forced or shamed into joining the local unit of the National Liberation Front. So afraid of their captors were these youthful warriors that they often disclosed locations of weapon caches or even underground tunnels to the interrogators. Their Ho Chi Minh style black "pajamas," floppy cotton hats, and sandals, often made from recycled tire treads, both amazed and amused curious onlookers.

Defiance exhibited by the highly trained, professional North Vietnamese soldier, on the other hand, often stirred emotions of anger and contempt among those caring for the patient as well as among nearby watching staff. The green canvas Russian-made uniform and the paper-pressed pith helmet with its five-pointed star insignia symbolized to many the mutilation and even death of so many young Americans. It was not difficult to hold this man personally responsible for killing the 18-year-old from Arizona brought in dead two days ago, or for setting the mine that took both legs from a youngster from Hawaii, or for throwing the grenade whose fragments paralyzed a father of two. Tried and convicted in the eyes of all present because of a uniform and an attitude!

※※※※※※

Not all of our patients, however, wore uniforms. Vietnamese civilians, from nine months to ninety years of age, would occasionally be brought from nearby villages after being caught in any one of a number of evil scenarios.

A toddler, without shoes and dressed only in a tee shirt, once appeared, the front of his tiny body peppered from head to toe with fragments. He probably tripped a booby trap that could well have been a Claymore mine, packed with over 700 steel pellets and planted in a field by allied forces months or even years earlier.

I recall a frail old woman, her back sprayed with fragments from a North Vietnamese mortar received while tending water buffalo in a field. Over and over in a high pitched yet feeble voice she cried, "Bac Si, Bac Si" (Doctor, Doctor). All the while she clung tightly to the straw conical hat used to shield her face from the sun.

Old men fared no better. Their gums purple and teeth blackened from years of chewing beetle-nut made them appear more exhausted and beaten from years of dealing with Vietcong "tax-collectors" and North Vietnamese soldiers who pillaged their homes of rice, and their animal pens of chickens and pigs. Most discouraging, however, was the fact that they dressed as did the Vietcong, in the traditional peasant black "pajamas." If caught in the "free fire zone" where only the enemy was supposed to be, they became instant targets for any and all allied forces. Likewise, helicopter door gunners, not rarely, fired on them as they ran for cover from rice paddies or open fields. High-velocity weapons and the age of these victims often led to their demise.

******

Because of an overstaffing of operating room nurses, and the periodic shortages of emergency room nurses, I was given the opportunity to work in both areas during my tour at 2nd Surg. And while I helped care for the "bad guys" in both assignments, in addition to our troops, there were "good guy" memories as well.

One of the top among those wearing the "white hats" was a 27-year-old Montagnard, meaning "mountain people" in French. With darker skin and having no epicanthic folds around their eyes, these people were often shunned by the mainstream Vietnamese. These Central Highlands tribesmen were, nonetheless, considered staunch American allies.

Our patient was raised in one of several longhouses in his village, sharing living space with 20 or so members of his immediate and extended family. He had little formal education and as a teen had helped his family in their quest of slash-and-burn farming, growing coffee and rice and raising buffalo, cows, pigs, and chickens. He harvested wild herbs and hunted wild game with a crossbow in nearby forests.

Shortly after marrying a girl from a neighboring tribe, taking her name, and moving into her family's longhouse as dictated by custom, their lives were disrupted when parts of the Ho Chi Minh Trail, the North Vietnamese supply line to the south, was developed not 100 yards from their village.

Soon, North Vietnamese soldiers traveling the trail began to plunder the village, rape the women, and execute men who protested. In an effort to resist, this man, along with other tribesmen, began to lie in wait, assassinating Vietcong and North Vietnamese regulars, sniper-style, with their crossbows. Gradually, he turned to aiding Special Forces in setting up base camps in the area, eventually fighting alongside our own troops.

In contrast to Washington's vaguely understood and never fully accepted attempt to contain global communism, this man's fight was as black and white as good and evil. As opposed to saving the world, his was a fight to keep his plot of land, preserve the honor of his wife, and earn respect for his culture. Known simply as "Yard," he had gained the respect of all who carded for him from admission to discharge.

******

Another good guy was a man much like Santa Claus in that he made his rounds only once a year. Not wearing the traditional red and white suit, he wore a Hawaiian shirt and carried a golf club. Bob Hope's arrival was always highly anticipated from the DMZ in the north to the Mekong Delta in the south.

In late 1967, Hope's Christmas USO tour packed Chu Lai's hospital outdoor theater with over 10,000 patients, staff, and U.S. and allied forces from all around the area. The war was put on hold for three or four hours, while the audience was entertained by Raquel Welch, Martha Raye, and, of course, Les Brown and his "Band of Renown."

While Hope's presence showed his support for the troops, his antics also helped dispel the homesickness they felt, and, for the moment at least, helped the troops forget the danger around them. Most of his jokes made light of the war. Some even touched on the controversy at home. "I bring you news from home," he said. "The country is behind you 50%."

Hope, however, wasn't without his share of critics. Editorials in stateside papers began taking pot shots at the generous paychecks coming from the U.S. government for these holiday junkets.

Suggestions were also being made that performances were only being given in totally secure areas of the country, thereby denying the front line troops of the entertainment.

Regardless of the adverse comments from the press, not a "Hawk" could be found, nor a "Boo" heard from any member of the crowd that day. Entertainers and audience alike knew they were well within mortar range of any Charlie in downtown Chu Lai. Somehow they put that thought aside and in unison, concluded the show with a resounding rendition of "Thanks for the Memory."

******

The color's fading, but I still have a few pictures of Bob Hope at Chu Lai. They're tucked away in an old shoebox somewhere. When I come across them, I remember a man who made one day in a horrific year more bearable.

I'm also able to put a face with a name when I stumble upon a tarnished brass friendship bracelet in the bottom of my jewelry box. Given to me by Yard during his hospitalization, I can still recall his dark skin, jet black hair, and cheerful smile. These and a few other "trophies" remind me of a few of the pleasant moments during the war.

On the other hand, I have no pictures of the men for whom I was sent to care for in Vietnam. I do remember, however, starting IVs on dozens of men whose bodies were riddled with mine fragments, and who clenched their teeth tightly rather than cry out with pain. I recall the courage it took for soldiers simply to slide from the stretcher to the operating room table as I supported their mutilated limbs or tortured bodies. I even occasionally think about those whose hands I held as they died.

It's probably a good thing I have no photos of these guys. While the mementos I do have remind me of happier times, having none of those who suffered from the constant misery allows me to detach myself somewhat from the very painful memories. With no pictures of faces to recall and no names to remember, the pain eases a bit. However, in all honesty, of all the people I've met, these will be the ones I'll find impossible to forget.

Chapter Nine

The Things You See

I suppose there are a hundred and one things you expect to see if you've been thrown into the middle of a war. There are probably just as many that in your wildest dreams, you'd never imagine possible. Flares, frag wounds, amputations, and AK-47s I assumed would be a part of everyday conversations. However, deaths from phosphorous burns and friendly fire were never listed in my welcome brochure to this part of the world.

My first surprise lay stacked on the tarmac at the Chu Lai airport on the day of my arrival in country. It was only natural that they be there, but the six or seven shiny silver-metal coffins, nonetheless, stopped me in my tracks. Impatiently, the men who had unloaded the coffins from the several nearby "cracker-box" ambulances were awaiting our deplaning so that they might load their charges for the first leg of their trip home. Here I was, sent to aid in the preservation of life, and my first impression of Vietnam was that of death.

The unexpected continued to happen, at any time, in any place. It didn't matter where you were, inside or out, day or night, in the operating room or even receiving; the shockers just kept popping up.

On a quiet Sunday morning, while some were attending services in our little grass shack of a chapel, and others were simply catching an extra forty winks, an eighteen-year-old, who would later die, was brought to Receiving. Both of his hands and one of his legs had been blown away by a booby trap. His chest and face had been pelted with shrapnel and blackened from the explosion. The force of the detonation had been so powerful that it had actually ripped his dog tags from around his neck. On the stretcher, lying at his side, was his boot, splintered bone and tattered muscle projecting from his foot, which was still inside.

Traumatic amputations were not uncommon, but the sight of the boot at the soldier's side made many uneasy. Some in the room, however, knew exactly why it was there.

Grunts, fearful that mines could literally blow them into a million pieces, that the dog tags around their necks could become lost in the dense jungle, and that in the chaos of battle and evacuation, their remains might never be identified, chose to double the odds that the latter would never happen. By wearing one dog tag around their neck and tying the other into the laces of a boot, chances were that their families would come to know their son, brother, or husband as a casualty of this war rather then missing in action for what could be an eternity. By placing his boot with the dog tag at his side, the comrades of this soldier were trying to assure that his family would know the truth. This action proved that the simplest of ideas are often born of necessity.

A North Vietnamese soldier also became the focus of attention when he arrived in Receiving, for one reason - because he had three or four through-and-through gunshot wounds of the chest and was still alive. Though a small miracle, the soldier was, nonetheless, immediately classified as "expectant," and corpsmen gathered to move him to the back room.

Suddenly, something sticking from the pocket of his fatigue jacket caught the eye of all around, and slowly, deliberately, it was removed. To everyone's amazement it was a white business card boldly displaying the "Screaming Eagle" of the 101st Airborne, and wording below indicating it had been placed there by a member of the famed "Widow Makers Club." In all probability, the man who placed the card thought that the soldier was dead, but a medic, finding life in the individual, had him evacuated to the 2nd Surg. We found it ironic that folks on the same team were fighting the war in two completely different ways.

******

We all firmly believed that the ugly side of the war would stay far from our front door. Needless to say, such an assumption was seriously flawed.

On a cool morning in the heart of monsoon season, word spread through the hooches that an "interrogation" was about to begin. Old timers told us that, though rare, they did occur, and that we should keep an eye on the South China Sea.

Gunship activity from the nearby helipad seemed unusually brisk. Suddenly, one chopper taking off over the ocean failed to veer off after gaining altitude, and continued to drift slowly out to sea. Probably about half a mile out it began to hover, perhaps 200 feet above the water. Slowly, the side door facing the shoreline slid open, and within seconds a tiny speck of a man in black VC garb, hands tied behind his back, was obviously tossed from the aircraft.

We could barely see the splash he made, and, though we watched the water for the longest time, we knew for certain he would never surface. Our attention eventually returned to the hovering helicopter, and sure as hell, another VC, hands bound behind his back, came flying out the door!

Though some were horrified at what they saw, cheers could be heard up and down the row of hooches. We all understood that a Vietnamese interpreter was aboard the helicopter, and that VC were being "dispatched" until someone spilled the beans. We also knew that this might someday be classified as a war crime, but in our hearts thought such action justified. Two VC lives for perhaps ten Americans, or the limbs of twenty more, seemed at the time a fair deal.

✳✳✳✳✳✳

Months later, on an unusually mild night, with no patients in Receiving or the operating rooms, staff were busy performing the routine stocking and sterilizing, when the thuds of incoming could be heard in the distance. Meandering outside, we could see the fiery explosions reflecting off low-lying clouds, but were unable to see the exact point of impact.

Climbing on crates, we made our way to the top of the Central Supply Quonset hut. From there we could see what appeared to be hit-and-miss mortar fire falling on the Marine base about two miles away. Home to a squadron of F-4 Phantom jets, it was becoming a favorite target of the Vietcong living in and around Chu Lai.

Pilots scurried for their aircraft, but time was running out as Charlie was beginning to zero in on the far end of the runway. The sound of outgoing artillery in the distance, however, gave promise that spotters had found and would silence the source of the barrage.

It soon looked like a game of "chicken" as pilots kicked on the afterburners and lifted the noses of their planes, bolting down the runway as mortars closed the gap by ten or fifteen yards at a time from the other end. Suddenly, the next jet in line to take off burst into an incredible ball of fire. Within seconds, the wing of another plane exploded and began to burn.

From our vantage point we could barely make out the flashing lights of the fire trucks, but patiently watched until the flames turned to darkness. At the same moment we became aware of the quiet. We realized the enemy activity had ceased. Regardless, it was now time to climb down from the rooftop and prepare for the casualties we had just seen inflicted.

✳✳✳✳✳✳

A few months later, the assault on the Marine base seemed like small potatoes when compared to the first night of the Tet Offensive. We had just turned off the lights in the hooch, when we felt an explosion so powerful that beds and lockers actually shimmied across the floor. The eyelids of all of us would-be dreamers opened wide. We gazed through the screening in amazement at what appeared to be an atomic bomb blast. Three of us remained frozen in position, but Pete had no hesitation about darting across the hooch and literally tearing the back door from its hinges as he headed for the hitherto-unused bunker. We later learned that the VC had targeted the main ammo dump. That was just the beginning of the festivities for the night.

Explosions followed explosions. Shortly, there was standing room only in the bunker. Accustomed to the relative safety of the hospital compound, however, folks began returning to their hooches once the noise and fires had subsided. Unaware of the full scope of the attack, most crept back to bed for what they assumed would be an uninterrupted snooze 'til dawn.

Heads had hardly hit pillows, however, when small arms fire brought all quickly to their feet again. From the next hooch you could hear, "The gook bastards are on the helipad!" And there they were. Seven or eight VC, black pajamas and all, not 500 yards away, spread out and running among the gunships and Dust-Offs. Some were returning fire at American guards trying to bring them down. Others were placing satchel charges inside or under choppers, setting the fuses, and scurrying to the next helicopter.

With this intense activity, hooches again emptied, and the bunker quickly filled to capacity. Rifle and automatic weapon fire became more frequent. We could hear choppers being blown to smithereens. Gradually the explosions ceased, and gunfire waned. Within ten or fifteen minutes, the only activity on the helipad was that of fire trucks dousing the flames, and GIs removing the bodies of dead VC.

By now it was well past 3 a.m., but few could return to sleep. Coffee pots perked in most hooches as small groups of men gathered on the walkways to watch the helipad cleanup and dwindling fires at the ammo dump. Dust-Offs in ever-increasing numbers began to break the quiet of the night. Soon surgeons were being called to care for casualties, and nurses to supplement the night staff. Within hours, radios all over the hospital were blaring with reports on what seemed to be the beginning of an enemy offensive. By dawn we learned that most district and provincial capitals were under attack. We knew that this would be a long day, but probably not our longest. We also knew that this day would somehow change the course of the war.

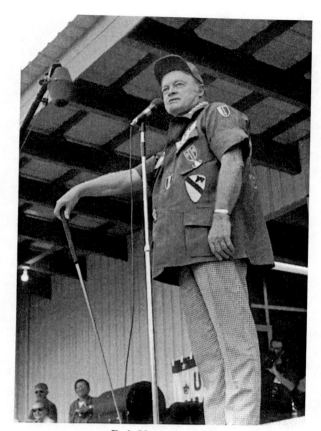

Bob Hope at Chu Lai

Mama-San

Montagnard Tribesman

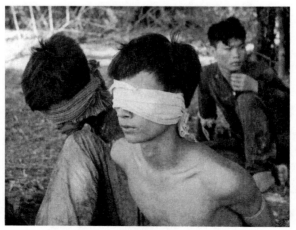

Vietcong POWs

Booby trap casualty

Outgoing mortars

Body count

Enemy strike on fuel depot

Chapter Ten

Reality Check #2

After five or six months in country, every soldier was entitled and encouraged to take a short breather known as R&R. It was five glorious days of rest and relaxation with free air transportation provided. Best of all, it was out of Vietnam!

Troops couldn't go home, but they had their choice of traveling to such exotic places as Australia, Bankok, Tokyo, Hong Kong, or Taipei. Through a small stroke of genius, the military had also authorized Hawaii as an R&R site, but solely for married men and women. Being the closest to the mainland, it was the cheapest location to which spouses could travel. However, though it had numerous hotels, its available accommodations would have been insufficient to meet the needs of thousands upon thousands of single soldiers.

When my R&R dates finally rolled around, the country and the hospital were smack dab in the middle of what was being called the Tet Offensive. We had no idea at the time how long this "push" would last, and since we were adequately staffed and my wife's airline tickets from the mid-west were non-refundable, higher-ups decided that I should set out for Hawaii as planned.

So, feeling a bit guilty (just a bit, mind you), I anxiously squeezed a swimsuit, shower clogs, and little else into a small bag, and began my trip by heading north to Da Nang. Here I was scheduled for an overnight stay in transient quarters, followed by an early-morning departure for the Paradise Islands of the Pacific.

While fatigues could be worn for comfort on the C-130 hop from Chu Lai to Da Nang, wearing a Class A or neatly starched dress uniform was required on the commercial flight to Hawaii. However, with luggage limited to one bag and no hanging garment bags allowed, for all practical purposes, we were forced to wear our Class As for both legs of the trip. With so little space to tuck away fatigues and combat boots, and no way to hang our dress uniform, it meant arriving in Honolulu with wrinkles galore. Nevertheless, this was the only sensible alternative.

Arriving in Da Nang in late afternoon, I took the opportunity to eat dinner on my way to the transient officers quarters. Like those in Chu Lai, they were simply a row of about a dozen wooden and screened hooches, each crowded with six or eight bunks with a chair at the foot of every bed. Connecting each hooch with the others was the customary wooden crate walkway. Running along the entire outside length of the walkway, a head-high chain link fence separated the hooches from a rice paddy on the other side. As usual, at each end of the row of hooches stood several covered sandbag bunkers.

As hooches filled, men quickly stripped to their skivvies in hopes of avoiding further crumpling of their khakis. With shirts and pants hung on chair backs, the plan for all was to wile away the time by reading, snoozing, and daydreaming of upcoming reunions.

Suddenly a wave of excitement began to spread from hooch to hooch. A young man in Air Force fatigues was going door to door announcing that he was a bus driver making courtesy runs to the White Elephant, the immense and highly acclaimed Da Nang Air Force Officers Club. Though it meant again dressing, and adding to our uniform wrinkle count, the temptation was irresistible. The chance to have a few draft beers or decent mixed drinks certainly entered our minds, but the opportunity to rub elbows with men other than those we'd been living with for the past six months promised to be a most welcomed diversion.

So, off we went, primed and ready to watch women, spout sports, and tell tall tales. We even tried for a few hours to forget where we were, and it worked - for a while.

The White Elephant was all it was advertised to be! It was huge, with bars as far as the eye could see, and bartenders more than happy to keep your glass full. There was laughter from every nook and cranny, and smiles just as plentiful. The brightly lit jukebox blared songs by The Four Tops, The Four Seasons, and Every Mother's Son. At one brief moment, every person in the club was doing the Twist. The war, its politics, and its pain seemed thousands of miles away as shooting the breeze focused on hometowns, the very first Super Bowl, and a hilarious new TV show known as Laugh-In.

Conversations slowly shifted to shop talk, however, as jocks in flight suits recounted the need to sweep low to dump their napalm on a suspected NVA base camp, and the maneuvers required to dodge a fast approaching surface to air missile. Eventually, the VC, NVA, and POWs were the only topics of discussion heard amidst the many pockets of partygoers.

Halfway through a song by Martha and the Vandellas the jukebox came to a sudden, horrible, screeching halt. As all eyes turned toward it, a big burly MP with plug in hand asked for everyone's attention.

"All right folks, listen up, please," he said. "I know we've been through this a thousand times before, but tonight's a bit different, trust me."

The regulars, knowing what was coming, gathered their money, and finished their drinks.

"This is no ordinary alert," he went on to say. "The base is being hit from all sides, and being hit hard. We need all transient personnel to immediately board the waiting buses outside the club, and Da Nang personnel to hunker down in bunkers nearest your quarters."

Our night of merrymaking had ended. The ride back was an eye-opener, with explosions from incoming rockets lighting up the night sky. From any window on the bus we could see huge rising orange and red fireballs, signifying direct hits on aircraft, ammo dumps, and napalm caches. Flares, meant to deter the enemy, lit up the entire perimeter of the base, but incoming strikes continued at an unrelenting pace. The drag race back to our assigned bunkers by our bus driver was most appreciated, as the war was now becoming a bit too close, a bit more intense, and quite frankly, downright scary.

The barrage lasted about an hour. After an hour of quiet, the standing-room-only crowd in our bunker was allowed to return to the hooches. No sooner had we all begun to get comfortable, however, when thunderous attacks began anew, and our trek back to the bunkers was again underway.

Again, an hour of Charlie lighting up the night, and an hour of calm, and a cautious return to our hooches. Exiting the bunker this time, however, we were told that because the night was young, and since the activity was likely to continue, we should sleep in our uniforms to allow for a rapid return to the bunkers. Though fully understanding the practicality of doing so, the idea of arriving in Hawaii in a uniform looking as though it had been picked from a rag bag was most unappealing. Everyone agreed, however, that it was the best choice. Everyone except me, that is.

Assuming the enemy had packed it in for the night, and under cover of darkness, I quietly undressed and again neatly hung my uniform across the back of a chair. Confident that I would awaken to bright sunshine and the excitement of seeing my wife for the first time in a long time, I squeezed beneath the mosquito netting and snuggled between the clean, cool sheets for what I was sure would be a night of safe, sound slumber.

I was dreaming, I'm sure, of sun and sand, of Mai Tias and hula girls, when the thunder of screaming incoming rockets literally shook the doors on the hooch, as well as the bed beneath me. Far closer than I'd ever heard them, the tremendous noise of the explosions and the sound of debris falling all around us quickly brought the fear of God into my heart.

I knew that bed was not the place to be at that precise moment, but in the same instant realized that my pants were on the chair. As hoochmates flew by, I slid from under the mosquito netting, and began to fumble blindly in the dark for my trousers. Ironically, a bursting mortar provided just enough light to allow me to reach my goal.

Suddenly, the frequency of incoming rockets doubled, the sounds of their blasts grew much louder, and the detonation flashes became even brighter. With one leg in my pants I tried desperately to place the second inside and to run at the same time. Again and again I struggled unsuccessfully, until soon I found myself outside the hooch, pants around my knees, and facing the bunker far in the distance - alone. I tasted supper in my throat, felt my heart pounding in my chest, and loudly cursed myself.

With pants unzipped, but finally up around my waist, I began to scramble along the wooden walkways as fast as my scrawny legs would carry me. Coming from behind, and in the rice paddy beside me, I could now hear and feel the shells falling faster than I could run from them. After twenty or thirty yards, the trembling ground made running unsteady. After about forty yards, chunks of mud began pelting the fence beside me. Thoughts of some "fastest scalpel" in this neck of the woods digging shrapnel out of my back began flashing through my brain.

Halfway to the bunker my luck seemed to be running even thinner, when the force of a concussion and the spray of debris knocked me off stride and up against the side of a hooch. Certain that the next rocket had my name on it, I began to question whether the Man Upstairs was simply testing my faith or, perhaps, trying to teach me a valuable lesson. "Dear God," I thought, "there has to be an easier way!"

In the next few seconds, a thousand ugly images streaked through my mind as I now seemingly accepted the possible consequences of my situation. I could see plainly my legs blown away; being carried on a stretcher, blood dripping from the canvas in steady streams. I knew I'd never see my wife again, and I even imagined being wheeled into and left alone in a "back room" somewhere.

I feared the pain, certainly, but I most dreaded the idea that I'd now be treated as just another casualty of this senseless war. I hated the thought I'd be seen as simply a body full of shrapnel on an operating room table, or another whining amputee complaining of phantom pain. I prayed that the nurses would lend a hand to squeeze if the pain got unbearable, would smile when I told them my daughter was in her "terrible twos," and had in fact heard loud and clear the Chief Nurse's charge that, "Without caring, you're useless to your patients."

I knew now that I had reached a level of fear that I had never thought possible. I screamed in my mind that I was a nurse, and the father of a soon-to-be-born son, and, damn it, here are my dog tags with my name on them!

Suddenly it occurred to me that continuing to run might not be in my best interest. On the other hand, ducking into an empty hooch to whose front screen I was steadfastly clinging seemed to be an attractive alternative. As I decided to head for the front door, however, I realized that the shells that had been creeping up behind me had now passed. Forty, then sixty, and soon a hundred yards beyond, they fell harmlessly into the rice paddy.

So, with grass in my hair and globs of mud on my bare back, I peeled my trembling body from the screening and began the long, lonely walk to the bunker. I was dreading the hassle I'd take from the guys when I got there, but I was actually more concerned with the fact that I'd almost "bought the farm." I appreciated that Charlie's aim was a little off that night, and that I had run a hundred yards in record time, but I also realized that I was within a few steps of experiencing what many of my patients had gone through. That terrified me.

It was near dawn before we were finally allowed to return to our hooches. I remember little of the rest of the night other than fumbling my way in the dark to the frigid shower to wash away the mud. I also recall sitting on my bunk or standing outside the hooch having a cigarette, bound and determined not to wrinkle my uniform, but, I'd be damned, awake and ready to run for that bunker if necessary.

✳✳✳✳✳✳

I LOVED Hawaii!! It was beautiful and pleasantly warm, and being with my wife again was like having a second honeymoon. We did the tourist things - buying flowered shirts, going to traditional luaus, and sipping drinks by the pool. We even found time to have dinner under the stars, and quiet morning walks on the beach.

We talked incessantly about the kids, parents, assignments after the war, the snow at home, and a thousand other tidbits. We touched on the war, certainly, and about the long hours, the water rationing, and the guys in my hooch. I swore up and down that I was faithfully taking my malaria pills. I described the difference in the sounds of incoming and outgoing, but assured my wife that the noise was always too far away to be of concern.

I never told her, of course, about my mud bath a few nights before. My idea was that telling served no purpose. Similarly, I never described in detail the horror of caring for teenagers whose bodies had literally been torn to pieces, and never shared the painful memories of befriending a patient who was destined to die.

As the precious days with my wife slipped away, I realized that I had forgotten the smells of 'Nam, of the operating rooms, and of rubber body bags. I could no longer hear the sounds of small arms fire, or incoming, or patients screaming for mercy. I was thankful for the reprieve, but at the same time knew I'd be returning to that world of chaos and killing in a matter of days.

Draped in aloha leis by the staff, we enjoyed our last dinner at the hotel followed by one final moonlit walk on the beach. Then, after talking half the night away, we stubbornly agreed to finally give in to the sleep we both so badly needed, but saying so and doing so were two different stories.

Lying on my back, I tried in vain to doze by watching the slowly spinning ceiling fan, but its only effect was to act as a background for pictures being painted in my mind. Row after row of sawhorses with stretchers holding bleeding GIs, a soldier walking off a helicopter holding his intestines in his hands, another holding his amputated arm. One after the other they became visible and then faded like flashbacks in an old movie. Sinking quickly into my brain was the fact that tomorrow they would have names. Tomorrow they would have faces.

Chapter Eleven

The Operating Room

From the outside it was nothing more than an old dilapidated wooden building. Hanging precariously from its ugly green peeling walls, about every fifteen or twenty feet, were rusty room-size air conditioners. They hummed constantly and dripped the humidity they removed from inside into puddles in the dirt below. Inside were the operating rooms - four, to be precise - surrounded by a myriad of small dressing and storage rooms, hallways, and rickety wooden ramps leading to adjacent buildings.

One ramp led to Central Supply, where surgical instruments were processed and sterilized. Another led to x-ray, from where most patients were sent to surgery immediately after films had been taken. The last was a steep downward slope from Receiving from where, of course, the most urgent patients came. Patients awaiting their turns on the surgical schedule also took this route, following the x-rays and preparation for surgery completed by the Receiving staff

Entering the operating rooms, you immediately knew that you were far from a stateside surgical suite. Fifty-five gallon drums, cut in half, open side up, took the place of shiny, stainless steel scrub sinks. Dim light bulbs hung where you might expect bright fluorescent lights. Rolling shadowy spotlights replaced the tremendous candlepower of modern overhead surgical lights. The operating table was manually operated, not electrically operated. The anesthesia machine was merely functional, not the "Cadillac" models found at home. Air conditioning was window-style as opposed to central air.

The story of these Operating Rooms, however, really can't be told simply with comparisons of esthetics, but rather by looking at any twenty-four hours within their walls. Then, and only then, can you truly have a feel for the level of care provided to each and every patient passing through their doors.

******

Like the day in the main room in Receiving, the day in the Operating Rooms began at 7 a.m. If all was quiet, the change of shift would find the thick black coffee from nights being replaced with a more palatable pot, and staffs casually giving and receiving reports. Notable in their conversations were comments that there were no size seven-and-a-half surgical gloves or embolectomy catheters (used to remove blood clots), that the sterilizers couldn't be run until gasoline was delivered, and that an air conditioner in one of the rooms was broken. The list went on and on and certainly changed from day to day, but oncoming nurses and technicians had little time to concern themselves with problems that over time had simply become a way of life.

Soon, men began pouring into Receiving after one had tripped one of those ever-popular booby traps on morning patrol. The operating room supervisor, who had traveled to Receiving and conferred with the triage officer following his initial assessments of patients, returned to the department and began to assign teams to rooms. Three or four staff were committed to open a room for a patient coming directly from Receiving, while two staff were earmarked to each of the remaining rooms for those making the short stop in x-ray. Before each team was dispatched, however, it received its patient's name and rank, names of surgeons assigned to its room, and the likely order of procedures to be performed.

Technicians briskly began their surgical scrubs, as circulating nurses opened prearranged packs and instrument sets. Within minutes the technicians were gowned and gloved. Soon thereafter, the first patient, still lying on the stretcher on which he was brought in, but now resting atop a gurney, was wheeled to rest beside the operating table in the room awaiting his arrival.

Again, as was typical of these patients, one leg was blown away just above the knee; the other was riddled with fragments that resulted in, among other things, several tears of the femoral artery. Fragments had also penetrated his abdomen, and his belly was slowly but surely filling with blood, probably from a lacerated liver or spleen. The list went on and on. The possible catastrophic consequences of all these injuries were mind boggling!

Following brief introductions, glimpsing at what little chart there was, the circulating nurse assured the patient he would not be moved from the stretcher to the operating table until he was asleep. The nurse anesthetist, between taking blood pressures, checking IV infusion sites, and pumping blood, informed the patient he was slipping him an intravenous "cocktail" to take the edge off the pain. The scrub technician, in the middle of hastily arranging his instrument table, caught the patient's eye, winked confidently and said, "Hang in there, sarge."

Despite the drugs, the pain was still so intense it caused the patient to dig his fingernails into the flesh of the nurse's hand he was holding. With assigned surgeons available, and the instrument set-up near completion, the anesthetist took this cue to induce the patient with sodium pentothal. Slowly the patient released his grip on the circulating nurse, who in turn assisted with intubating the patient. Once this was accomplished, anesthesia was maintained with a mixture of halothane, nitrous oxide, and oxygen.

The staff cut the remaining mud-caked clothing away from the patient. Though tourniquets stemmed the flow of blood from both legs, so much blood had oozed from the dressings and other wounds that it had seeped through the stretcher, run off the gurney onto the floor, and made the floor extremely slippery. Despite the difficult footing, however, four or five pairs of hands slid beneath the patient's head, back and legs to lift him from the blood-soaked stretcher to the operating table.

This patient, like so many, would require the skills of several specialty surgeons. In this situation, a general surgeon, assisted by a second general surgeon, would first perform an exploratory laparotomy to find and halt the cause of the abdominal bleeding. A vascular surgeon, probably assisted by one of the general surgeons, would then repair the arterial damage to the "good" leg. Next, an orthopedic surgeon would revise the traumatic amputation. Finally, the two general surgeons would return to work simultaneously to debride the multiple fragment wounds on the patient's trunk, arms, hands, and face. Because he was wearing a flak jacket, his chest had no wounds, and more importantly, because of the flak jacket, his life had been spared.

As the general surgeons performed their surgical scrubs, circulating nurses and technicians began to prep the patient using an iodophor. The scrub technician paused just long enough to gown and glove the surgeons, but quickly returned to complete the instrument set-up.

The staff strictly adhered to sterile technique as they placed sterile drapes beneath the patient's legs. Sterile towels isolated the tourniquets and the patient's groin from the operative fields. Finally, top and side towels and drapes framed his abdomen and excluded his chest, head, and arms.

Instrument trays and tables were pushed into position as the operative team gathered around the patient, and all eyes met to indicate their collective readiness. The hiss of the deflating blood pressure cuff, and the anesthetist's "OK, folks," signaled his approval to begin.

The laparotomy proceeded with amazing rapidity. These highly qualified surgeons were backed by a skilled technician who simply watched and listened in order to anticipate their needs; heavy absorbable suture on blunt needles for liver repairs, bowel clamps for resection where the blood supply has been impaired, or silk sutures to close small bowel perforations. Furthermore, knowing that air evacuation was apt to aggravate abdominal distention, and that intestinal repairs mandated their use, abdominal retention sutures and wire sutures to close muscle were on hand long before they were needed.

******

Once the patient's intra-abdominal problems had been resolved, attention quickly shifted to his damaged femoral artery. While the vascular surgeon used finely crafted vascular clamps and modern vascular sutures, the similarities with "stateside" surgery began to disappear, and the uniqueness of combat surgery emerged.

The mine that had disfigured this man now determined variations in otherwise routine operative procedures. The contents of such booby traps were hand-picked by the enemy to ensure that if the device didn't kill his foe, it would greatly impede his recovery. Rusty chunks of jagged metal, wood and glass, all liberally doused with cow manure, were all favored to pack these iron blockbusters.

It was obvious that this patient's wounds were contaminated and potentially infected. For this patient the implications were many. The first was to empty the vascular surgeon's toolbox of artificial grafts that might otherwise replace a torn-a-way segment of the patient's femoral artery.   Champions at harboring microorganisms leading to life threatening situations, their use was forbidden.   Additionally, both saphenous veins, each potential arterial substitutes, were identifiable only as parts of mutilated tissue masses that had to be radically excised. Conservatism was frowned upon, since even the smallest amount of remaining necrotic tissue favored infection-producing bacteria.

Physician ingenuity, provided the few extra centimeters needed to achieve an end-to-end anastomosis (re-connection of the severed artery) by flexing the patient's hip and knee and tunneling the tattered ends of the artery anterior to its original route. The repair was then covered with transposed muscle to prevent dehiscence (bursting out of the artery), and the soft tissue above debrided and covered with fine mesh gauze and dressings. A rigid posterior splint would maintain this position until conditions favored the insertion of an artificial graft.

******

With the battle to save one leg concluded, the orthopedic surgeon moved quickly to revise the end of the patient's splintered femur. The surgeon performed an open circular amputation with the incision several inches above the stump. A lower level of amputation might have been possible, but the skin and tissue above the stump had been devitalized for several inches. All vessels were ligated (tied off) as encountered, and all major nerves transected as far superiorly as possible without traction. With bleeding controlled, fine mesh gauze was applied to the stump, which was then loosely packed with fluffed gauze. Liquid adhesive was then applied to the skin above the stump and stockinet applied. The stump was then wrapped with compressive bandages and traction applied to the end of the stockinet. The hope was that this continued traction would result in the skin eventually closing over the end of the stump, eliminating the need for subsequent skin grafting procedures.

Last, the general surgeons returned, debrided the remaining numerous fragment wounds of all devitalized tissue, and controlled bleeding. Left open, the wounds were simply covered with fine mesh gauze and dressings to await delayed primary closure in four or five days when the risk of infection was greatly reduced.

※※※※※※

Similar scenes were occurring in all the operating rooms. In one, doctors debrided and splinted a tibial fracture that, under ideal conditions, would have been reduced and fixated with plates and screws. Again, the introduction of a foreign body was contraindicated because of the increased risk of infection. In another room, the positions of severed peripheral nerves were noted, but repairs were not attempted. Further dissection to expose nerve endings would only have extended the area of contamination with possible irreversible consequences. Constantly, the physicians altered surgical techniques to minimize the possible devastating effects of pathogens, now embedded in debris and nurtured on a diet of necrotic tissue.

Soon the three rooms with less seriously injured soldiers began to "break," while the surgery on the most critical patient continued for several more hours. Scrub technicians carried instruments to Central Supply, where they were hand washed, sorted, assembled into sets, and sterilized. Circulating nurses helped each other clean and restock rooms. They opened sterile packs as the next patients arrived, and a replay of the previous fight for life and limb began anew.

Morning turned to afternoon, and while the pace didn't change, the type of wounds encountered did. Afternoon patients had engaged the enemy in "fire fights," and high-velocity AK-47 rounds caused bones to shatter, shocked arteries to thrombose, and nerves to snap from waves of pressure. Entrance wounds were minuscule, while exit wounds were massive, with extensive damage in between. Head wounds were common; thoracotomies a frequent procedure for chest wounds; and paralyzing spinal cord injuries seen far too often.

Dusk found the day shift physically beat and emotionally drained. Backs ached and feet inside their bloody sneakers were dog tired, yet not one soul complained. Most had missed supper, but some were already planning on late night C-rations as soon as they hit the hooch; others, a few beers and peanuts at the club.

The flood of patients slowed to a trickle, with two of the operating rooms closed and the other two on their last cases. Staff not with patients kept busy cleaning and stocking the two empty rooms from top to bottom including, scrubbing blood from spotlights, tables, walls and wheels. Finally, mopping the floor and the dozens of dried bloody footprints seemed to be the final piece in the puzzle of removing the smell of war from the air - a smell that was a kind of humid mixture of grit, grime, gunpowder, and blood.

Nurses scurried to complete paperwork as cases wound down in both remaining rooms. Moments before physicians began to apply dressings, anesthetic agents were discontinued, and pure oxygen administered to assist the patient in awakening. The focus of attention remained on the patient as the circulating nurse stood at his side, offering a firm hand of reassurance; at the same time, deep sighs of relief could be heard from all around the room. Tired and sweaty, surgeons flopped onto stools to write post-op orders, while the scrub technician slouched wearily over the instrument table.

It was about 6:30 p.m., then quarter to seven, and, like angels from heaven, members of the night shift began to appear. Enthusiastically, they immediately pitched in, breaking down instrument tables and cleaning rooms, while the day shift nurses assisted with taking patients to the recovery room. They knew from the log book that all four operating rooms had been running constantly the entire day. Patients had facial reconstructions and fractured femurs; bowel repairs, bowel resections, and bowel exteriorizations; nephrectomies (kidney removals), spleenectomies (spleen removals), and pneumonectomies (lung removals); and a list of misery that went on forever. In addition, after many hours and countless pints of blood, two young men had lost their lives.

The night crew also knew that theirs was apt to be a busy shift, at least early on. Word from Receiving was that a Dust-Off was minutes from the hospital with four wounded on board. Typical of the hit-and-run tactics of the Vietcong, these men had been injured when the enemy lobbed several mortars into their base camp as they settled in for the night. Fiery fragments had riddled their bodies, and the endless devastation of this bloody stalemate had once again reared its ugly head.

Because the number of casualties treated at night was usually much fewer, staff hospital-wide were reduced accordingly. Unsure of the needs of the incoming patients, however, and with night staff only able to run two operating rooms, the day shift lingered until patients' needs were assessed and staffing requirements established. Until then, all worked side by side, cleaning and setting up the two recently vacated rooms.

******

Darkness fell and the staff from the day shift had finally retired to their hooches or headed for an impromptu meeting of the Journal Club. Enemy activity had ceased, but Receiving staff were kept on their toes, and the operating rooms kept running, with an "accidental" gunshot wound of the foot, a stabbing at a local club, and two drunk GIs rolling a jeep.

On most nights, the wee hours of the morning were quiet, allowing staff to play catch up. Linen packs had to be made, hundreds of liters of saline irrigating solution prepared, instruments cleaned and assembled into sets, laparotomy sponges wrapped, and all had to be sterilized before the next wave of patients arrived in a few hours.

Finally, time permitting and if someone remembered, someone dumped the pot of black sludge, and brewed fresh coffee. With batteries recharged, the same personnel, relieved only hours before, returned for a new day of trying to put all the pieces back together. The only difference was that on this day, they would have new names and new faces.

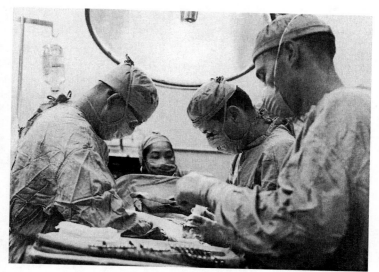
Surgical scene

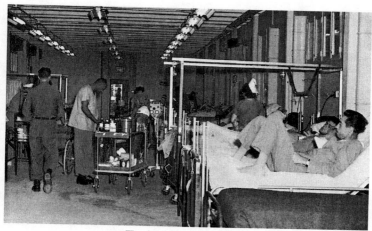
Typical hospital ward

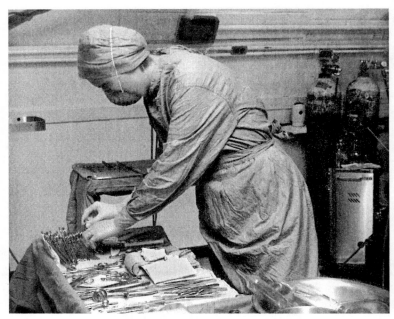

Operating Room instrument set-up

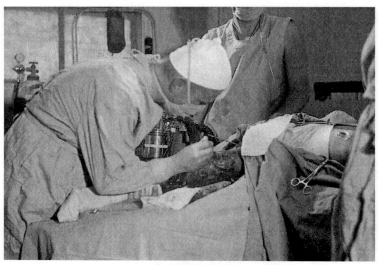

Arm and chest debridement

Chapter Twelve

The Journal Club

It wasn't as if, after a hard day at the office, you could go home to your wife and complain that you never got your full hour for lunch or would never see the overtime in your paycheck. It wasn't as if you could think about calling in sick the next day, or even consider a career change in the near future. So, without the ability to go home and kick the dog or call and fake the flu, there had to be an opportunity to vent your own frustration or listen to someone else's; to share feelings of anger or fear; or simply, to share the difficulty of dealing with the day-in and day-out horrors of this hell on earth.

It was called the Journal Club, held anywhere, anytime, with three people or ten, and was considered by all as the next best thing to a psychiatrist's couch. Gatherings most often convened following a fourteen or fifteen-hour-long day shift, when most staff had no lunch, and gobbled down what little supper they could in ten or fifteen minutes. These were usually the same days when casualties were not only the heaviest, but with the most severe injuries; the same days when more than a few men died.

Meetings, of course, were never formally announced. Word simply spread by grapevine. Usually a group of nurses would meander into the Officers Club or a hooch, incredibly exhausted, but rarely too tired to miss these sessions. After all those grueling hours it was time to sit back, kick off your boots, and talk frankly about what went on that day.

Chatter filled the room. Everyone obviously felt anxious to begin. Questions began flying before the tabs had even been popped on all the beer cans.

"Did the kid shot in the chest this afternoon make it?" someone asks.

From somewhere at the table came a muffled and clearly disappointing, "No."

"How about the guy who stepped on the land mine this morning?"

"Yablonski? Yeah. He's doing pretty well," was the reply.

Back and forth the queries come at a blistering pace.

"Any word on the redhead shot in the back?"

"Not yet. We'll try to call the hospital ship in the morning, but he wasn't moving anything when we flew him out, so it doesn't look good."

Though a bit enthusiastic at the start, the meetings were not, as might appear, simply a means of compiling a tally of wins and losses. Eventually the pace would slow, and questions and answers would become a back-and-forth sharing of ideas, a dialogue of sorts, seeking to validate and improve individual and group efforts of that day. It was always an open and honest discussion on how to do things better; never an exercise in finger pointing, though at times a most humbling experience.

Topics for these powwows ranged from anatomy and physiology of thoracic injuries, to caring for patients with inhalation burns, to those "million dollar" wounds that would get GIs sent home without killing them. Receiving nurses jostled between themselves as did operating room nurses, but most conversations followed a specific patient from the front door of Receiving to the operating room to his bed on the ward.

From a nurse anesthetist, "Do you think you could have gotten a bigger intravenous catheter into the guy with the liver and spleen injuries?"

The Receiving nurse, "I don't think so. His blood pressure was pretty low, and I didn't want to miss, and blow any chance of getting in."

Finally from an operating room nurse, "You're pretty damn good at starting IVs. I think next time you should try a 14 gauge as opposed to the 16. You'll get it, and you know how much of a difference it'll make on how fast we can pump blood.

******

The primary concern for all nurses, of course, was to do first things first, but to do them well. Something as simple as applying a tourniquet, or what instrument sets were opened in the operating room, were cause for critique.

Placing a tourniquet on a patient, for example, with a traumatic amputation below the knee required that it be done once, correctly. Applying it in haste, however, over the patient's uniform, guaranteed unequal pressure distribution, possibly making it ineffective. In addition, it would have to be removed later in the operating room to allow for prepping the leg for surgery. Here the tourniquet would have to be removed, clothing cut away, padding applied to the patient's thigh, and the tourniquet reapplied all with the patient under anesthesia. It would have been in the best interest of the patient if this task was performed correctly the first time.

Opening instrument sets in the operating room in a timely manner was also a critical task. An example might be opening intestinal instruments when a patient was scheduled for an exploratory laparotomy and possible bowel resection. With 50% of all laparotomies performed on suspicion of bowel perforations being negative, opening the intestinal instruments meant at the minimum re-wrapping and re-sterilizing them. If unused, the additional work would certainly be unnecessary, but if water or gasoline were unavailable to run the sterilizers, it put patients yet to arrive at risk because sets would be unavailable to meet their needs. In this situation, simply having the set available but unopened in the room solved the problem.

******

A thousand and one similar scenarios were put under the microscope during these sessions. A few became quite spirited. None, however, were more passionate than when the emotional trauma inflicted on patients, and perhaps shared equally by staff, came bubbling to the surface.

"What the hell do you say to a kid who just had his balls blown away," snapped one Receiving nurse.

"How do you answer to, Lieutenant, am I dying?" asked another.

A third jumped in with, "A guy with both arms and half his face blown away asked me what he had to do to die."

Operating room nurses were just as vocal, but with a slightly different view.

One said, "Today we patched up the same damn soldier for the third time in four months. He'll go home now because it's his third Purple Heart, but it gets me sick that we fix them up just so they can go back out in the jungle, and try to get killed again. And for what?"

Yet another related, "Ya know, we used fifty-five pints of blood on the guy with the vena cava gunshot wound today, and lost him. I probably spent two minutes with him, and spoke maybe thirty words before we put him to sleep. I never saw his face again once surgery began because of the drapes, and when he died I thought since I hadn't gotten to know this guy, it really wouldn't bother me. Yeah, right! When we undraped him, and I saw his young face drained of all color, it felt like I had lost my closest friend. It hurt like hell!"

✳✳✳✳✳✳

The Journal Club may not have been the most appropriate name for these meetings, as there were no books to review, or even read for that matter. Nonetheless, whether they were held in the Officers Club with an attendance of twelve after a long day, or in a hooch with three after a brutal night, they served their purpose well.

There were no professors to share their wealth of knowledge, nor students taking notes, but these sessions were a classroom in the truest sense of the word. Nurses eagerly soaked in the expertise shared by old timers, and old and young alike vigorously debated introducing new ways of doing things as opposed to the tried and true methods.

Receiving nurses talked about tubes and trachs, mortality rates, grateful smiles between grimaces of pain, the cries of dying teens, and bravery. Operating room nurses touched on getting the sponge count correct, how some things were repaired, and why others were removed, the endless line of patients, the cries of dying teens, and bravery.

Of course, none of the world's problems were ever solved at any of these Journal Club meetings. In fact, many of the questions were never answered. It was at these times, however, that all could share the emotional consequences of having befriended, no matter how briefly, a dying or mutilated soldier. It was these times, also, that all could recall names and faces, remember the agony that went with them, and share in the pain of doing so.

Chapter Thirteen

Homeward Bound!

It was early morning, probably about eight o'clock, and already unbearably hot and humid. I remember sitting on my bunk and staring blankly into a small trash can, empty except for a so-called "Short-Timer Calendar" I'd just thrown into it. On it I had scratched off that day, just like the days before it, in anticipation of my departure from Chu Lai. The days over the past month had seemed to pass unmercifully slowly, but at long last the big day had arrived. I was going home!

In my daze I was remembering coffins on the tarmac, a nineteen-year-old who had dared to die in the back room almost a year ago, and Pete and the "fastest scalpel in the whole of Vietnam," now both long gone. As if in another world, I could barely hear the roaring blades of a landing Dust-Off, and began to picture in my mind patients being carried up the dusty ramp into Receiving. These mutilated men I would never meet; never share their pain, and this for some reason brought a deep sigh of relief.

At the same time I also realized I was alone. The world as I knew it was at work, knee deep in blood, and I was no longer a part of it. The farewells had come and gone; the tears, the hugs behind me. The men I had come to know better than my own brother, and loved just as much, were out of sight, and quickly becoming out of mind. For a brief moment, however, I struggled with desires of continuing these friendships as opposed to totally erasing all memories of this hellhole. Thankfully, the "beep, beep, beep" of my ride to the airport finally brought me back to reality. Hurriedly I gathered duffel and ditty bags to begin the first leg of my trip back to the "real world."

From here I was heading south, two hundred miles to Cam Ranh Bay. As its name implies, and like Chu Lai, it was also adjacent to the South

China Sea. Opened in the mid-1960s as a convalescent center, it accommodated patients requiring extended hospitalization, but who return to duty within sixty days of injury. Now, because it was approximately equidistant from bases in the north and south, on the coast, and had an airport, it was also being used as an embarkation point for troops heading home. Here I'd tarry for a few days, updating payroll and personnel records, and finalizing connecting plane reservations home once our military flight arrived in Seattle. These were to be days of breathing easier, gradually unwinding, and mounting anticipation.

In contrast to the uniform nightmare of my Hawaiian R&R, this leg of the journey promised to be one of far less tension, and considerably more physical comfort. For starters, I could travel and process out at Cam Ranh Bay in combat fatigues, far more appealing than trying to maintain a wrinkle-free appearance in Class As. Furthermore, before departing, I could at my leisure, burn or bury these very same fatigues, leaving behind the feel, the smell, in fact the war.

******

Cam Ranh Bay was still the Army, still Vietnam, and still in the middle of the cruelest of wars; however, it was considered extremely safe because of its location, size, number of troops both on and around the base, and the presence of the hospital, seldom attacked by the enemy for fear of retaliation on their own. It was no wonder that steel helmets were few and far between, and finding someone wearing a flak jacket next to impossible.

Cam Ranh Bay also seemed to be serving as a site for reorientation to civilization. There were flush toilets, hot and cold spigots atop white porcelain sinks, and hot showers whenever you cared to take one. There were also signs of what was and what was to be. Grunts, in an almost religious ceremony, could be seen removing the dog tag laced deep in their boot, and placing it around their neck with its mate for the first time in a year. At the same time, nurses strolled the grounds in starched white uniforms, a reminder of days to come.

What processing had to be done was performed quickly and efficiently.

Doing so allowed time to have our Class As cleaned and pressed; to get a decent haircut; to exchange script for dollars; and most important, to relax. The Officers Club, of course, the very place for that!

So, like every other officer heading home, I, too, headed for the club. Meandering up to the bar, I grabbed the first empty stool, ordered my brew, placed my money on the bar, and slowly turned my head. Four men on my right, who up until now had been laughing loudly, fell silent, their mouths now open, and staring in my direction. Instantly smiles came to all of our faces. It was impossible not to remember these men, who, with me, had buried the fear of coming here with a few days of heavy drinking and raising hell in San Francisco. It was a glorious moment!

A year earlier, knowing what little I knew about helicopter pilot survival statistics, and the fact that the war was heating up, I would have given even odds that one of these guys would have gone home in a box. I, of course, had been protected beneath those big red crosses atop the Quonset huts, and honestly expected to be where I was at that moment. These men, though, had literally passed through the fiery gates, and were here because of a combination of their bravery and pure luck.

One of the men had been awarded the Silver Star for bravery, landing in a hot LZ to pick up a squad surrounded by Charlie. Another had been shot down, and rescued only after spending several days in the jungle. The third was embarrassed to admit he had received the Purple Heart by taking a round through his seat in his chopper, and into his butt. The last man never got a scratch, but one of his co-pilots and one of his door gunners were killed on two separate occasions.

This was not a night, however, to relive the highlights of a few disastrous moments of the year gone by. Instead it was a night on which to begin a celebration of our escape from this insanity known as 'Nam. No one was to speak of artillery or amputations, of napalm or gunships. No one was permitted to utter the words Charlie, gook, or Vietcong the entire night. No one could mention hours in bunkers or days without mail. The law of the land on this night was to put it all behind us!

The club was packed with people and loud talking, laughing, and the booming of the juke box. Bartenders rolled their eyes as if to say, "Where have I heard this before," as they eavesdropped on men scheming to surprise loved ones on their arrivals home. For the hundredth time in as many nights they overheard plots of scurrying up on the front porch of a childhood sweetheart, carrying a dozen red long stem roses, or sneaking through the back door as the wife and kids were sitting down to dinner. One creative individual even planned on ringing the doorbell while announcing himself as the Avon Lady!

The mood remained upbeat the entire evening, helped along, no doubt, by the tremendous amount of alcohol being consumed. Men drank freely because they could sleep that night, unafraid for the first time in a year of being awakened, and told to grab a rifle and man the perimeter, man an artillery post, fly a mission, or staff an operating room. It was a night's sleep they had consciously anticipated, elated that it had finally arrived, but not yet ready to pack it in for the night and cut off those indescribable feelings they were experiencing for the mere pleasure of laying their head on a pillow.

As the hours passed, and the imbibing continued, the ability not to relive time spent in 'Nam as promised earlier in the evening became increasingly more difficult. Though the reminders felt painful, relating small anecdotes from the past year appeared cathartic to story teller and listener alike. One final recollection, for example, of "Willie Peter" or white phosphorous mortars exploding violently around them proved to be, for some, a dramatic, though, I suppose meaningful attempt at trying to shake the past. Using terms never again to be repeated such as "White mice" (the South Vietnamese police who wore white helmets and gloves), "Dinky dau" (crazy), or "choke" (peanut butter), seemed to me a bit more whimsical method of trying to do the same.

It was evident that these men had served their time in hell, and each to the other were reliving their darkest hours interspersed with a few amusing moments. For most, memories recalled in this room on this night of a meaningless war and its unacceptable costs were to be blotted out and lost for all time. The killing, the tracers, the rockets, the blood, and the thousands of other sights and sounds were all to be forgotten like so many dreams.

As this was also my last night in this miserable little corner of the world, I, too, became a part of this undertaking. Knowing that I had made a difference, and that many young men, even in death, were aware of my touch, I could now at least try to leave behind the memories of mutilated young bodies, bloody boots, and dying cries. I knew, I knew deep in my soul, that maybe not today, but tomorrow, tomorrow for sure, I'd begin to forget the names. Likewise, I was sure I'd begin to forget the faces, and just maybe that would help erase the pain of dealing with the hurt and loss. Just maybe the pain would go away. Just maybe.

Epilogue

In the ten or so years of the Vietnam war, slightly over 6,000 nurses cared for well over a quarter of a million soldiers, many standing at their side as some of the more than 58,000 closed their eyes for the last time. It was a herculean task performed with competence and compassion, but occasionally paid for at an exceptionally high emotional cost.

Friendships in 'Nam developed quickly; some superficial, some remarkably genuine and incredibly strong. All were based on trust. Certainly grunts trudging through the jungle relied heavily on their point man, as did pilots on their co-pilots, or patients lying on a stretcher staring up into the eyes of a nurse.

When such friendships were wobbled by horrifying wounds or even death, reactions varied widely depending on the degree of attachment, and nurses were no different in their responses than any other soldier. They, too, struggling to care for an endless line of mutilated and dying young men, faced the same emotional chaos as their caring became feelings, and their feelings turned to pain.

Time, they were told, would erase that pain; names would be forgotten, and eventually faces would fade from their memories. The reality of it, however, was that dealing with those memories would be a battle lasting well beyond the end of the war, and evidence is demonstrated with a visit to the Vietnam Memorial in Washington, D.C. Here, aging men with pot bellies and "Vietnam Veteran" baseball caps weep openly as they stroll past the names of fallen comrades etched in the brilliant black granite. Voices and sounds of the war echo in their minds and faces seen only by them are reflected from deep within the towering stone wall. For these men, the war goes on. For all the men and women who served the conflict continues. For grunts, helicopter pilots, and nurses, alike, the friendships never end, and the faces never fade. The names are permanently etched in stone and the pain is forever.

About the Author

After serving for 23 years in the Army Nurse Corps, John Kildea retired and moved to York, Pennsylvania, where he continues to work in the nursing field. He is the author of many articles published in nursing and medical journals. *No Names, No Faces, No Pain*, a memoir of his year as an operating room nurse in Vietnam, is his first book.